D1014073

Thinking through Sources for
Exploring American Histories

Volume 1: To 1877

Thinking through Sources for
Exploring American Histories

Volume 1: To 1877

Second Edition

Nancy A. Hewitt
Rutgers University

Steven F. Lawson
Rutgers University

bedford/st.martin's
Macmillan Learning
Boston • New York

For Bedford/St. Martin's

Vice President, Editorial, Macmillan Learning Humanities: Edwin Hill
Publisher for History: Michael Rosenberg
Senior Executive Editor for History: William J. Lombardo
Director of Development for History: Jane Knetzger
Developmental Editor: Jennifer Jovin
Assistant Editor: Mary Posman
Senior Production Editor: Gregory Erb
Media Producer: Sarah O'Connor
Production Coordinator: Carolyn Quimby
Executive Marketing Manager: Sandra McGuire
Photo Researcher: Christine Buese
Permissions Editor: Kalina Ingham
Senior Art Director: Anna Palchik
Text Design: Lily Yamamoto, LMY Studios
Cover Design: William Boardman
Cover Art: View of Baltimore, c. 1850 (oil on canvas), Lane, Fitz Henry (1804–65) / Private
    Collection / Bridgeman Images
Composition: Cenveo Publisher Services
Printing and Binding: RR Donnelley and Sons

Manufactured in the United States of America.

11   10   9   8   7   6
f   e   d   c   b   a

For information, write: Bedford/St. Martin's, 75 Arlington Street, Boston, MA 02116
(617-399-4000)

ISBN 978-1-319-04237-0

Acknowledgments
Art acknowledgments and copyrights appear on the same page as the art selections they cover.

John Ross, *The Papers of Chief John Ross, Volume 1, 1807–1839,* ed. Gary E. Moulton. Copyright © 1985 University of Oklahoma Press. Republished with permission from University of Oklahoma Press; permission conveyed through Copyright Clearance.

Ella Gertrude Clanton Thomas, *Secret Eye: The Journal of Ella Gertrude Clanton Thomas, 1848–1889* (Chapel Hill: University of North Carolina Press, 1990).

PREFACE

"History," Mark Twain reputedly said, "doesn't repeat itself, but it does rhyme." While Twain was not suggesting that the past was poetry or the lyrics of a song, he did recognize that historical events create echoes that continue to resonate into the present. To hear and decipher those sounds across the centuries, scholars and students must listen carefully to the chorus of voices that, taken together, provide a soundtrack of American histories. Of course, not all voices rhyme perfectly with other voices, and there are also harsh and dissonant voices. The document projects in this reader allow us to hear many different sounds as we seek to interpret particular moments in the American past.

This reader for the second editions of *Exploring American Histories* and *Exploring American Histories,* Value Edition, consists of a series of document projects each of which contains four or five documents of different types from different viewpoints focused on a particular event, issue, or development at key points in U.S. history. The document projects follow the chapter structure of *Exploring American Histories* and are styled like the projects in the full version of the textbook. The sources include maps, personal letters and diaries, memoirs, advertisements, posters, cartoons, government reports, speeches, trial testimony, song lyrics, and laws. The roster of historical figures represented in these sources includes well-known individuals and organizations as well as ordinary women and men. The document projects range, for example, from "Mapping America" to "Homefront Protest during the Civil War" in Volume 1 and from "Women in the West" to "The Environment and Federal Policy in the Twenty-first Century" in Volume 2. The project on "Reconstruction in South Carolina" appears in both volumes. Each project includes a brief introduction and headnotes to the primary sources followed by five "Interpret the Evidence" questions and one or two "Put It in Context" questions. These questions encourage students to recognize connections among documents and relate the sources to larger historical themes. Students must also consider the range of sources, the quality of evidence in each source, and the relevance of that evidence to the questions and the larger context as they analyze the documents and build an interpretation.

The reader is available in both print and electronic formats and is built into the LaunchPad for *Exploring American Histories* so that you and your students can access the documents wherever and whenever it is convenient for you. If you choose to pair LaunchPad with your print books, students will have access to multiple-choice quizzes for the documents and our new "Thinking through Sources" pedagogy, which consists of two auto-graded activities at the end of each project that ask students to make supportable inferences and draw appropriate conclusions from sources with reference to a guiding question. "Thinking through Sources" culminates in a set of essay questions that build upon the historical arguments students developed in the auto-graded activities. It is through reading and analyzing the documents that students will begin, as Mark Twain might have put it, to hear the rhymes of the past in the present.

GUIDE TO ANALYZING PRIMARY SOURCES

In their search for an improved understanding of the past, historians look for a variety of evidence—written documents, visual sources, and material artifacts. When they encounter any of these primary sources, historians ask certain key questions. You should ask these questions too. Sometimes historians cannot be certain about the answers, but they always ask the questions. Indeed, asking questions is the first step in writing history. Moreover, facts do not speak for themselves. It is the task of the historian to organize and interpret the facts in a reasoned and verifiable manner.

Analyzing a Written Document

- What kind of document is this? For example, is it a diary, letter, speech, sermon, court opinion, newspaper article, witness testimony, poem, memoir, or advertisement?
- Who wrote the document? How can you identify the author? Was the source translated by someone other than the author or speaker (for example, American Indian speeches translated by whites)?
- When and where was it written?
- Why was the document written? Is there a clear purpose?
- Who was, or who might have been, its intended audience?
- What point of view does it reflect?
- What can the document tell us about the individual(s) who produced it and the society from which he, she, or they came?
- How might individuals' race, ethnicity, class, gender, and region have affected the viewpoints in the documents?
- In what ways does the larger historical context help you evaluate individual sources?

Analyzing a Visual or Material Source

- What kind of visual or material source is this? For example, is it a map, drawing or engraving, physical object, painting, photograph, or political cartoon?
- Who made the image or artifact, and how was it made?
- When and where was the image or artifact made?
- Can you determine if someone paid for or commissioned it? If so, how can you tell that it was paid for or commissioned?

- Who might have been the intended audience or user? Where might it have originally been displayed or used?
- What message or messages is it trying to convey?
- How might it be interpreted differently depending on who viewed or used it?
- What can the visual or material source tell us about the individual who produced it and the society from which he or she came?
- In what ways does the larger historical context help you evaluate individual sources?

Comparing Multiple Sources

- In what ways are the sources similar in purpose and content? In what ways are they different?
- How much weight should one give to who wrote or produced the source?
- Were the sources written or produced at the same time or at different times? If they were produced at different times, does this account for any of the differences between or among the sources?
- What difference does it make that some sources (such as diaries and letters) were intended to be private and some sources (such as political cartoons and court opinions) were meant to be public?
- How do you account for different perspectives and conclusions? How might these be affected by the author's relative socioeconomic position or political power in the larger society?
- Is it possible to separate fact from personal opinion in the sources?
- Can the information in the sources under review be corroborated by other evidence? What other sources would you want to consult to confirm your conclusions?

Cautionary Advice for Interpreting Primary Sources

- A single source does not tell the whole story, and even multiple sources may not provide a complete account. Historians realize that not all evidence is recoverable.
- Sources have biases, whether they appear in personal or official documents. Think of biases as particular points of view, and try to figure out how they influence the historical event and the accounts of that event.
- Sources reflect the period in which they were written or produced and must be evaluated within the historical time frame from which they came. Explain how people understood the world in which they lived, and be careful to avoid imposing contemporary standards on the past. Nevertheless, remember that even in any particular time period people disagreed over significant principles and practices such as slavery, imperialism, and immigration.
- Sources often conflict or contradict each other. Take into account all sides. Do not dismiss an account that does not fit into your interpretation; rather, explain why you are giving it less weight or how you are modifying your interpretation to conform to all the evidence.

CONTENTS

DOCUMENT PROJECT

Mapping America

As Europeans expanded their trade and exploration in the fifteenth century, they gathered information about navigational routes and the regions they encountered. Cartographers used this information to create increasingly accurate maps of the known world. One of the leading efforts in mapmaking was conducted under the leadership of Prince Henry of Portugal. His assemblage of cartographers, geographers, astronomers, and explorers helped revolutionize European understandings of the western coast of Africa and nearby islands in the Atlantic. The 1513 Piri Reis map (Document 1.2), in particular, used Portuguese maps to chart Africa and the Atlantic.

Columbus's discovery of the Western Hemisphere in 1492 redrew the map of the world. Although he believed he had found a route to Asia, by 1507 when the *Universalis Cosmographia* appeared, cartographers understood this as an entirely new region. Throughout the early sixteenth century, maps of the Americas continued to expand and modify knowledge of what was termed the "New World," whose territory would be claimed by Spain, Portugal, England, France, and other European powers. Of course, the Western Hemisphere was not a "new" world but instead one inhabited by millions of indigenous peoples with complex societies of their own. Document 1.4 is an example of a map created by indigenous people in what is now Mexico; they often used maps not only to depict an area but also to record developments in that region that had occurred over decades or even centuries.

The following maps depict changing understandings of Europe, Africa, and the Americas from 1490 to the mid-sixteenth century, as well as the increasing interconnectedness of these regions. They represent not only attempts to chart territory and navigational routes but also cultural beliefs about the world and the people encountered by Europeans. As you examine them, think about what their creators chose to include, what they left out, and how these maps helped shape European attitudes toward Africa and the Western Hemisphere.

1

DOCUMENT 1.1 | CHRISTOPHER AND BARTOLOMEO COLUMBUS,
Map of Europe and North Africa (c. 1490)

While Christopher Columbus's discovery of the Americas is well-known, his younger brother Bartolomeo also played a part in the early discovery and exploration of the Western Hemisphere. Bartolomeo was a cartographer and navigator who accompanied Christopher on several explorations. This map is believed to have been produced in the Lisbon workshop of Christopher and Bartolomeo Columbus in 1490, two years before Columbus set sail on his first voyage. It depicts Europe and North Africa and also includes a circular world map on the left.

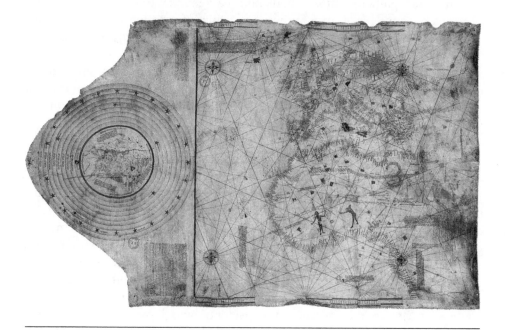

Library of Congress

DOCUMENT 1.2 | *Piri Reis Map* (1513)

The Turkish admiral and cartographer Piri Reis produced another early-sixteenth-century map. While much of the map does not survive, the remaining part includes the western coasts of Europe and North Africa, the eastern coast of South America, and the northern coast of Antarctica. Reis used Portuguese, Ptolemaic, and Arabic maps to produce his version of the world, and the illustrations are detailed and reasonably accurate.

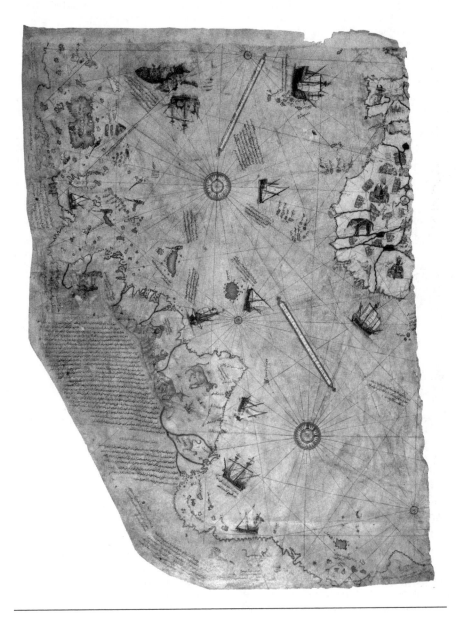

DOCUMENT 1.3 | *Dauphin Map of Canada* (c. 1543)

Although Jacques Cartier was not the first European to explore present-day Canada, he was the first to penetrate into the eastern interior, aided by two Iroquois guides whom he had kidnapped. The French explorer claimed the region for France in the 1530s, and over the next decade he completed three voyages to explore and map the Gulf of St. Lawrence region. He also sought what he believed were great riches at a legendary Indian kingdom named Saguenay. The map shown here, known as the Dauphin Map of Canada and based on Cartier's explorations, includes French Canada and the entire east coast of North America. Created in 1543, this map includes the largest Indian settlements (Hochelaga and Stadaconna) but also names and claims numerous rivers, inlets, harbors, and the lands surrounding them for the French. Finally, it also illustrates some of the land claims of England and Spain in the region.

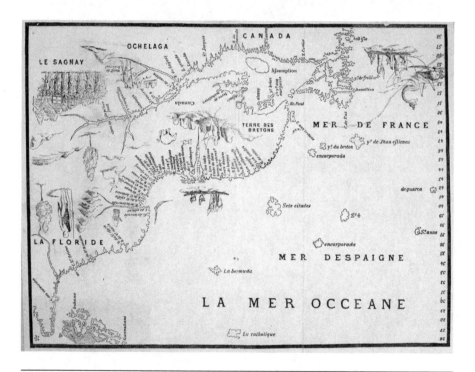

Library and Archives Canada

DOCUMENT 1.4 | *Map of Cuauhtinchan* (1550)

The *Historia Tolteca-Chichimeca* is a series of Nahuatl-language annals written in the mid-sixteenth century. Covering the history of the Cuauhtinchan region (in present-day Mexico) during the previous four hundred years, the text focuses mainly on the area's social and political history. Most of the narrative deals with events that occurred before, or were unrelated to, Spanish activity in the region. Illustrations accompanied the text, including the map shown here. This map, covered with some seven hundred glyphs, depicts how the Toltec-Chichimeca peoples of the Puebla valley left their seven-chambered cave of Chicomoztoc, conquered their enemies, and established their new home at Cuauhtinchan in 1183 C.E. Like many native maps, it combines myth and history with geography and tells a story across time and space. Yet this territorial map was considered so reliable that it was used as evidence in Spanish colonial courts in the sixteenth century.

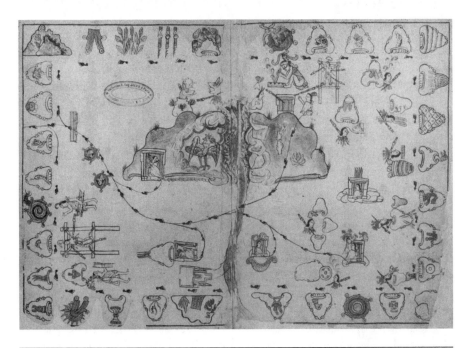

Nettie Lee Benson Latin American Collection, University of Texas Libraries, The University of Texas at Austin

INTERPRET THE EVIDENCE

1. How did the mapmakers who created Documents 1.2 and 1.3 represent the lands being discovered and claimed by various European nations?

2. What were the different purposes of the various maps included here?

3. What elements other than geographical features appear on these maps, and what were they intended to symbolize?

4. Compare the Cuauhtinchan map (Document 1.4) with those created by Europeans. What are the major differences? What do you think these differences reveal about the cultures of the mapmakers?

PUT IT IN CONTEXT

1. What are the strengths and weaknesses of modern mapmaking compared with older mapmaking?

2. What has been gained and what has been lost in the transition from one to the other?

DOCUMENT PROJECT 2

Comparing Virginia and Massachusetts Bay Colonies

The first English settlers who came to North America arrived with different goals. When John Smith (Document 2.1) and the Virginia Company landed in Jamestown in May 1608, they sought wealth and profit and hoped to extend the crown's imperial reach in the New World. Farther north about two decades later, the Puritans settled Massachusetts Bay to flee religious persecution. Under the leadership of Governor John Winthrop (Document 2.3), they hoped to set an example of godly behavior for the rest of the world, although they were not averse to achieving economic success as well. In both places, however, many colonists found that their lives were incredibly difficult. Food was scarce, sickness ran rampant, and colonists had to address the fact that the lands they claimed were already inhabited by Indians (Document 2.2) who would have a say in the future of both colonies. As Richard Frethorne (Document 2.4) and the son of William Pond (Document 2.5) learned, the realities of life in the colonies often failed to live up to the hopes of the colonists.

The following documents examine settlements in Virginia and Massachusetts Bay. As you read, consider not only the differences between the two colonies but also what they shared in common.

DOCUMENT 2.1 | JOHN SMITH, *The Commodities in Virginia* (c. 1612)

John Smith played a central role not only in founding Virginia but also in promoting the colony in hopes of attracting new settlers. In the following account, Smith describes the abundant resources that Virginia had to offer settlers in the 1600s.

The Commodities in Virginia, or that may be had by Industrie.

The mildnesse of the ayre, the fertilitie of the soyle, and situation of the rivers are so propitious to the nature and use of man, as no place is more convenient for

---

Source: Edward Arber, ed., *Captain John Smith of Willoughby Alford, Lincolnshire; President of Virginia and Admiral of New England, Works: 1608–1631* (Birmingham: The English Scholar's Library, 1884), 359–60.

pleasure, profit, and man's sustenance, under that latitude or climat. Here will live any beasts, as horses, goats, sheepe, asses, hens, &c. as appeared by them that were carried thether. The waters, Isles, and shoales, are full of safe harbours for ships of warre or marchandize, for boats of all sorts, for transportation or fishing, &c.

The Bay and rivers have much marchantable [commercial] fish, and places fit for Salt coats, building of ships, making of Iron, &c.

Muscovia and Polonia [Russia and Poland] doe yearely receive many thousands, for pitch, tarre, sopeashes, Rosen, Flax, Cordage, Sturgeon, Masts, Yards, Wainscot, Firres, Glasse, and such like; also Swethland [Sweden] for Iron and Copper. France in like manner, for Wine, Canvas, and Salt. Spaine asmuch for Iron, Steele, Figges, Reasons, and Sackes. Italy with Silkes and Velvets consumes our chiefe Commodities. Holland maintaines it selfe by fishing and trading at our owne doores. All these temporize [traffic] with other for necessities, but all as uncertaine as peace or warres. Besides the charge, travell, and danger in transporting them, by seas, lands, stormes, and Pyrats [pirates]. Then how much hath Virginia the prerogative of all those flourishing Kingdomes, for the benefit of our Land, when as within one hundred myles all those are to be had, either ready provided by nature, or else to be prepared, were there but industrious men to labour. Onely of Copper we may doubt is wanting, but there is good probabilitie that both Copper and better Minerals are there to be had for their labour. Other Countries have it. So then here is a place, a nurse for souldiers, a practise for mariners, a trade for marchants, a reward for the good, and that which is most of all, a businesse (most acceptable to God) to bring such poore Infidels to the knowledge of God and his holy Gospell.

DOCUMENT 2.2 | *Powhatan's Viewpoint, as Reported by John Smith* (1608)

The resources John Smith promoted in 1612 (see Document 2.1) were less apparent just a few years earlier. Upon arriving in Jamestown, Smith and the English colonists met the Algonquian chief Powhatan, who adopted a reluctant Smith as an Algonquian werowance, or chief. The Indians helped the colonists through their first brutal winters, but by 1608 the fragile alliance between Powhatan and Smith had begun to break down. The following document, recorded by Smith, reveals Powhatan's complaints.

Captaine Smith, you may understand that I having seene the death of all my people thrice, and not any one living of these three generations but my selfe; I know the difference of Peace and Warre better then any in my Country. But now I am old and ere long must die, my brethren, namely Opitchapam, Opechancanough, and Kekataugh, my two sisters, and their two daughters, are distinctly each others successers. I wish their experience no lesse then mine, and

Source: John Smith, *The Generall Historie of Virginia, New England & the Summer Isles: Together with the True Travels, Adventures and Observations, and a Sea Grammar* (New York: Macmillan, 1907). http://www.loc.gov/item/75320262/.

your love to them no lesse then mine to you. But this bruit[1] from Nandsamund,[2] that you are come to destroy my Country, so much affrighteth all my people as they dare not visit you. What will it availe you to take that by force you may quickly have by love, or to destroy them that provide you food. What can you get by warre, when we can hide our provisions and fly to the woods? whereby you must famish by wronging us your friends. And why are you thus jealous of our loves seeing us unarmed, and both doe, and are willing still to feede you, with that you cannot get but by our labours? Thinke you I am so simple, not to know it is better to eate good meate, lye well, and sleepe quietly with my women and children, laugh and be merry with you, have copper, hatchets, or what I want being your friend: then be forced to flie from all, to lie cold in the woods, feede upon Acornes, rootes, and such trash, and be so hunted by you, that I can neither rest, eate, nor sleepe; but my tyred men must watch, and if a twig but breake, every one cryeth there commeth Captaine Smith: then must I fly I know not whether: and thus with miserable feare, end my miserable life, leaving my pleasures to such youths as you, which through your rash unadvisednesse may quickly as miserably end, for want of that, you never know where to finde. Let this therefore assure you of our loves, and every yeare our friendly trade shall furnish you with Corne; and now also, if you would come in friendly manner to see us, and not thus with your guns and swords as to invade your foes. . . .

Captaine Smith, I never use any Werowance so kindely as your selfe, yet from you I receive the least kindnesse of any. Captaine Newport[3] gave me swords, copper, cloathes, a bed, towels, or what I desired; ever taking what I offered him, and would send away his gunnes when I intreated him: none doth deny to lye at my feet, or refuse to doe what I desire, but onely you; of whom I can have nothing but what you regard not, and yet you will have whatsoever you demand. Captaine Newport you call father, and so you call me; but I see for all us both you will doe what you list, and we must both seeke to content you. But if you intend so friendly as you say, send hence your armes, that I may beleeve you; for you see the love I beare you, doth cause me thus nakedly to forget my selfe.

DOCUMENT 2.3 | JOHN WINTHROP, *A Model of Christian Charity* (1630)

John Winthrop became governor upon the Puritans' arrival in Massachusetts, but he established his expectations for the colony before they made landfall. Winthrop gave the following sermon to fellow colonists aboard the *Arbella*, in which he outlined his plan for a new society that would serve as an example to the world.

Source: *Collections of the Massachusetts Historical Society*, 3rd ser., vol. 7 (Boston: Charles C. Little and James Brown, 1838), 44–47.

[1]**bruit**: Rumor.
[2]**Nandsamund**: A tribe of the Powhatan Confederacy.
[3]**Captain Newport**: Christopher Newport, British ship captain and privateer.

Herein are 4 things to be propounded; first the persons, 2ly the worke, 3ly the end, 4thly the meanes.

1: For *the persons*. We are a company professing ourselves fellow members of Christ, in which respect onely though we were absent from each other many miles, and had our imployments as farre distant, yet we ought to account ourselves knit together by this bond of love, and, live in the exercise of it, if we would have comforte of our being in Christ. . . . 2nly for the *worke* we have in hand. It is by a mutuall consent, through a special overvaluing of providence and a more than ordinary approbation of the Churches of Christ, to seeke out a place of cohabitation and Consorteship under a due form of Governement both civil and ecclesiastical. In such cases as this, the care of the publique must oversway all private respects, by which, not only conscience, but mere civil policy, doth bind us. For it is a true rule that particular Estates cannot subsist in the ruin of the publique. 3ly The *end* is to improve our lives to do more service to the Lord; the comforte and increase of the body of Christe, whereof we are members; that ourselves and posterity may be the better preserved from the common corruptions of this evil world, to serve the Lord and worke out our Salvation under the power and purity of his holy ordinances. 4thly for the *meanes* whereby this must be effected. They are twofold, a conformity with the work and end we aim at. These we see are extraordinary, therefore we must not content ourselves with usual ordinary meanes. Whatsoever we did, or ought to have done, when we lived in England, the same we must do, and more also, where we go. That which the most in their churches mainetaine as truth in profession onely, we must bring into familiar and constant practice; as in this duty of love, we must love brotherly without dissimulation, we must love one another with a pure hearte fervently. We must beare one anothers burthens. We must not look onely on our owne things, but also on the things of our brethren. Neither must we think that the Lord will beare with such failings at our hands as he dothe from those among whome we have lived. . . .

For this end, we must be knit together, in this worke, as one man. We must entertaine each other in brotherly affection. We must be willing to abridge ourselves of our superfluities, for the supply of other's necessities. We must uphold a familiar commerce together in all meekeness, gentlenes, patience and liberality. We must delight in eache other; make other's conditions our oune [own]; rejoice together, mourne together, labour and suffer together, allwayes having before our eyes our commission and community in the worke, as members of the same body. So shall we *keepe the unitie of the spirit in the bond of peace.* The Lord will be our God, and delight to dwell among us, as his oune [own] people, and will command a blessing upon us in all our ways. So that we shall see much more of his wisdom, power, goodness and truthe, than formerly we have been acquainted with. We shall finde that the God of Israel is among us, when ten of us shall be able to resist a thousand of our enemies; when he shall make us a prayse and glory that men shall say of succeeding plantations, "the Lord make it likely that of *New England.*" For we must consider that we shall be as a city upon a hill. The eyes of all people are upon us. So that if we shall deale falsely with our God in this worke we have undertaken, and so cause him to withdraw his present help from us, we shall be made a story and a by-word through the world.

DOCUMENT 2.4 | RICHARD FRETHORNE, *Letter Home from Virginia* (1623)

Most Virginia settlers found that life in the new colony did not live up to John Smith's ideal. For thousands of people in England, the only way to afford the trip to the New World was to travel as an indentured servant. These servants provided the labor that allowed tobacco planters to get rich, but they rarely earned much themselves. In the following letter, indentured servant Richard Frethorne describes the misery of his early days in Virginia.

Loveing and kind father and mother my most humble duty remembred to you hopeing in God of your good health, as I my selfe am at the makeing hereof, this is to let you understand that I your Child am in a most heavie Case by reason of the nature of the Country [which] is such that it Causeth much sicknes, as the scurvie and the bloody flix, and divers other diseases, wch maketh the bodie very poore, and Weake, and when we are sicke there is nothing to Comfort us; for since I came out of the ship, I never ate any thing but pease, and loblollie (that is water gruel) as for deer or venison I never saw any since I came into this land, there is indeed some fowl, but We are not allowed to goe, and get it, but must Worke hard both earelie, and late for a messe of water gruel, and a mouthful of bread, and beef, a mouthful of bread for a pennie loafe must serve for 4 men wch is most pitiful if you did knowe as much as I, when people cry out day, and night, Oh that they were in England without their lymbes and would not care to lose any lymbe to be in England againe, yea, though they beg from door to door, for we live in feare of the Enimy every hour, yet we have had a Combate with them on the Sunday before Shrovetyde, and we tooke two alive, and make slaves of them, but it was by pollicie, for we are in great danger; for our Plantation is very weake, by reason of the dearth, and sicknes, of our Companie, for we came but Twentie for the marchaunts, and they are halfe dead Just; and we looke every hour When two more should goe, yet there came some other men yet to live with us, of which there is but one alive; and our Lieutenant is dead, and his father and his brother, and there was some 5 or 6 of the last yeares 20 of wch there is but 3 left, so that we are faine to get other men to plant with us, and yet we are but 32 to fight against 3000 if they should Come, and the nighest help that We have is ten miles of us, and when the rogues overcame this place last, they slew 80 Persons how then shall we doe for we lie even in their teeth.

Source: Susan M. Kingsley, ed., *The Records of the Virginia Company of London*, vol. 4 (Washington, D.C.: Government Printing Office, 1935), 58.

DOCUMENT 2.5 | *Letter Home from Massachusetts Bay* (1631)

Just as settlers faced difficulties and disappointment in Virginia, New England often proved less than advertised. Even those driven by religious motivations still had to raise enough food to eat. The following letter from an unnamed English migrant in the settlement of Watertown in Massachusetts Bay colony, written in 1631 to his father, William Pond, reveals the economic issues that settlers faced and their perceptions of Indians.

I know, loving father, and do confess that I was an undutiful child unto you when I lived with you and by you, for the which I am much sorrowful and grieved for it, trusting in God that He will guide me that I will never offend you so anymore, and I trust in God that you will forgive me for it.

My writing this unto you is to let you understand what a country this New England is, where we live. Here are but few Indians, a great part of them died this winter, it was thought it was of the plague. They are a crafty people, and they will cozen and cheat, and they are a subtle people. And whereas we did expect great store of beaver, here is little or none to be had. . . . They are proper men and clean-jointed men, and many of them go naked with a skin about their loins, but now some of them get Englishmen's apparel. And the country is very rocky and hilly, and there is some champion ground, and the soil is very flete [fruitful]. And here is some good ground and marsh ground, but here is no Michaelmas. Spring cattle thrive well here, but they give small store of milk. The best cattle for profit is swine, and a good swine is here at five pounds' price, a goose is worth two pounds, a good one got. Here is timber good store, and acorns good store, and here is good store of fish, if we had boats to go for and lines to serve fishing. Here are good stores of wild fowl, but they are hard to come by. It is harder to get a shot than it is in old England. And people here are subject to disease, for here have died of the scurvy and of the burning fever nigh too hundred and odd. Besides, as many lyeth lame, and all Sudbury men are dead but three, and [some] women and some children, and provisions are here at a wonderful rate. . . .

If this ship had not come when it did, we had been put to a wonderful strait, but thanks be to God for sending of it in. I received from the ship a hogshead of meal, and the Governor telleth me of a hundred-weight of cheese, the which I have received part of it. I humbly thank you for it. I did expect two cows, the which I had none, nor I do not earnestly desire that you should send me any, because the country is not so [suitable] as we did expect it. Therefore, loving father, I would entreat you that you would send me a firkin of butter and a hogshead of malt unground, for we drink nothing but water, and a coarse clothe of four pounds price, so it be thick. For the freight, if you of your love will send them I will pay the freight. For here is nothing to be got without we had commodities to go up to the East parts amongst the Indians to truck, for here where we live, here is no beaver. Here is no cloth to be had to make no apparel, and

Source: *Proceedings of the Massachusetts Historical Society*, 2nd ser., vol. 8 (Boston, 1892–1894), 471–73.

shoes are at five shillings a pair for me, and that cloth that is worth two shillings eight pence a yard is worth here five shillings. So I pray, father, send me four or five yards of cloth to make us some apparel. And, loving father, though I be far distant from you, yet I pray you remember me as your child. And we do not know how long we may subsist, for we cannot live here without provisions from old England. Therefore, I pray, do not put away your shop stuff, for I think that in the end, if I live, it must be my living. For we do not know how long this planta-tion will stand, for some of the magnates that did uphold it have turned off their men and have given it over. . . .

So here we may live if we have supplies every year from old England, oth-erwise we cannot subsist. I may, as I will, work hard, set an acre of [English] wheat, and if we do not set it with fish (and that will cost 20 shillings), if we set it without fish, they shall have but a poor crop. So, father, I pray, consider of my case, for here will be but a very poor being—no being—without, loving father, your help with provisions from old England. I had thought to have come home in this ship, for my provisions were almost all spent, but that I humbly thank you for your great love and kindness in sending me some provisions, or else I should and might have been half famished. But now I will—if it please God that I have my health—I will plant what corn I can.

INTERPRET THE EVIDENCE

1. How does John Smith describe Virginia (Document 2.1)? According to Smith, what does Virginia have to offer settlers? Why do you think he wrote this docu-ment? What does he mean by "a businesse (most acceptable to God) to bring such poore Infidels to the knowledge of God and his holy Gospell"?

2. What are Powhatan's (Document 2.2) complaints of John Smith and the Eng-lish colonists? Does he support peace or war with the colonists? Considering that John Smith recorded the conversation, what might call into question its accuracy?

3. Why, according to John Winthrop, were the Puritans traveling to the New World (Document 2.3)? What obligations did the colonists have to one another? What did he mean when he said they would live as "a city upon a hill"?

4. How does Richard Frethorne describe his experience in Virginia (Document 2.4)? Whom does he refer to as "the Enimy"?

5. What problems did the settler in Watertown encounter (Document 2.5)? What was his opinion on the future of the settlement? How did he describe the Indians? How does his letter compare to Frethorne's letter? Why are these kinds of letters valuable to historians?

PUT IT IN CONTEXT

1. Based on what you have read, how did the colonies of Virginia and Massachu-setts Bay differ? In what ways were they similar?

The Atlantic Slave Trade

The trade in human cargo was central to European nations' larger Atlantic ambitions. British and Anglo-American ships alone brought three million slaves to the Americas between 1700 and 1808, when the international slave trade ended in the young United States. Africans who were captured from their homelands and sold to Europeans entered a world of horror. They crossed the Atlantic on overpacked slave ships, where a large percentage of them died before reaching their final destination. Those who did survive were consigned to lives of endless backbreaking labor in South America, the West Indies, or North America. This exploitation allowed European nations to solidify empires and to enrich plantation owners, seaport merchants, and slave traders.

The following documents—written by English and Dutch traders and the slaves themselves—explore the process of the Atlantic slave trade: the capture of the slave, the sale to European merchants, and the Middle Passage. As you read, consider who participated in the slave trade and why they did so. Think also about the ways in which enslaved people tried to come to grips with their grim fate.

DOCUMENT 3.1 | VENTURE SMITH, *A Narrative of the Life and Adventures of Venture, a Native of Africa* (1798)

Venture Smith was born to a West African prince in the first decades of the eighteenth century. At the age of six, he was captured and sold into slavery in North America. Thirty years later, he purchased his own freedom. The following excerpt from his memoir describes the events that led to his initial capture.

Not more than six weeks had passed after my return, before a message was brought by an inhabitant of the place where I lived the preceding year to my

Source: Venture Smith, *A Narrative of the Life and Adventures of Venture, a Native of Africa, But Resident above Sixty Years in the United States of America. Related by Himself* (New London, CT: C. Holt, 1798), 7–12.

father, that that place had been invaded by a numerous army, from a nation not far distant, furnished with musical instruments, and all kinds of arms then in use; that they were instigated by some white nation who equipped and sent them to subdue and possess the country, that his nation had made no preparation for war, having been for a long time in profound peace; that they could not defend themselves against such a formidable train of invaders, and must therefore necessarily evacuate their lands to the fierce enemy, and fly to the protection of some chief; and that if he would permit them they would come under his rule and protection when they had to retreat from their own possessions. He was a kind and merciful prince, and therefore consented to these proposals.

He had scarcely returned to his nation with the message, before the whole of his people were obliged to retreat from their country, and come to my father's dominions.

He gave them every privilege and all the protection his government could afford. But they had not been there longer than four days before news came to them that the invaders had laid waste their country, and were coming speedily to destroy them in my father's territories. This affrighted them, and therefore they immediately pushed off to the southward, into the unknown countries there, and were never more heard of.

Two days after their retreat, the report turned out to be but too true. A detachment from the enemy came to my father and informed him, that the whole army was encamped not far out of his dominions, and would invade the territory and deprive his people of their liberties and rights, if he did not comply with the following terms. These were to pay them a large sum of money, three hundred fat cattle, and a great number of goats, sheep, asses, etc.

My father told the messenger that he would comply rather than that his subjects should be deprived of their rights and privileges, which he was not then in circumstances to defend from so sudden an invasion. Upon turning out those articles, the enemy pledged their faith and honor that they would not attack him. On these he relied and therefore thought it unnecessary to be on his guard against the enemy. But their pledges of faith and honor proved no better than those of other unprincipled hostile nations; for a few days after a certain relation of the king came and informed him, that the enemy who sent terms of accommodation to him and received tribute to their satisfaction, yet meditated an attack on his subjects by surprise, and that probably they would commence their attack in less than one day, and concluded with advising him, as he was not prepared for war, to order a speedy retreat of his family and subjects. He complied with this advice.

The same night which was fixed upon to retreat, my father and his family set off about the break of day. The king and his two younger wives went in one company, and my mother and her children in another. We left our dwellings in succession, and my father's company went on first. We directed our course for a large shrub plain, some distance off, where we intended to conceal ourselves from the approaching enemy, until we could refresh ourselves a little. But we presently found that our retreat was not secure. For having struck up a little fire for the purpose of cooking victuals, the enemy who happened to be encamped a little distance off, had sent out a scouting party who discovered us by the smoke of the fire, just as we were extinguishing it, and about to eat. As soon as we had finished eating, my father discovered the party, and immediately began to discharge arrows at them. This was what I first saw, and it alarmed both me and the women, who being unable to make any resistance, immediately betook ourselves to the tall thick reeds not far off, and left the old king to fight alone. For some time I beheld him from the reeds defending himself with great courage and firmness, till at last he was obliged to surrender himself into their hands.

Then they came to us in the reeds, and the very first salute I had from them was a violent blow on the back part of the head with the fore part of a gun, and at the same time a grasp round the neck. I then had a rope put about my neck, as had all the women in the thicket with me, and were immediately led to my father, who was likewise pinioned and haltered for leading. In this condition we were all led to the camp. The women and myself being pretty submissive, had tolerable treatment from the enemy, while my father was closely interrogated respecting his money which they knew he must have. But as he gave them no account of it, he was instantly cut and pounded on his body with great inhumanity, that he might be induced by the torture he suffered to make the discovery. All this availed not in the least to make him give up his money, but he despised all the tortures which they inflicted, until the continued exercise and increase of torment, obliged him to sink and expire. He thus died without informing his enemies where his money lay. I saw him while he was thus tortured to death. The shocking scene is to this day fresh in my mind, and I have often been overcome while thinking on it. He was a man of remarkable stature. I should judge as much as six feet and six or seven inches high, two feet across his shoulders, and every way well proportioned. He was a man of remarkable strength and resolution, affable, kind and gentle, ruling with equity and moderation. . . .

On the march the prisoners were treated with clemency, on account of their being submissive and humble. Having come to the next tribe, the enemy laid siege and immediately took men, women, children, flocks, and all their valuable effects. They then went on to the next district which was contiguous to the sea, called in Africa, Anamaboo. The enemies' provisions were then almost spent, as well as their strength. The inhabitants knowing what conduct they had pursued, and what were their present intentions, improved the favorable opportunity, attacked them, and took enemy, prisoners, flocks and all their effects. I was then taken a second time. All of us were then put into the castle, and kept for market.

DOCUMENT 3.2 | THOMAS PHILLIPS, *Voyage of the* Hannibal (1694)

When European traders reached Africa, they engaged in often-protracted negotiations to acquire slaves. English slave trader Thomas Phillips, the owner and captain of the *Hannibal*, sailed to Africa in 1694. In the following excerpt from his log, Phillips explains his interaction with an African king and the complex process of purchasing slaves.

Source: Thomas Phillips, *A Journal of a Voyage Made in the* Hannibal *of London in 1694* (London: 1732), 216–18.

As soon as the king understood of our landing, he sent two of his cappasheirs, or noblemen, to compliment us at our factory [trading post], where we designed to continue that night, and pay our devoirs to his majesty the next day, which we signify'd to them, and they, by a foot-express to their monarch; whereupon he sent two more of his grandees to invite us there that night, saying he waited for us, and that all former captains used to attend him the first night: whereupon, being unwilling to infringe the custom, or give his majesty any offense, we took our hamocks, and Mr. Peison, myself, Capt. Clay, our surgeons, pursers, and about 12 men arm'd for our guard, were carry'd to the king's town, which contains about 50 houses. When we came to the palace (which was the meanest I ever saw, being low mud walls, the roof thatch'd, the floor the bare ground, with some pools of water and dirt in it) we were met at the entrance by several cappasheirs, with the usual ceremony of clapping their hands, and taking and shaking us by ours, with great demonstration of affection: when we enter'd the palace-yard they all fell on their knees near the door of the room where the king was, clapping their hands, knocking the ground with their foreheads, and kissing it, which they repeated three times, being their usual ceremony when they approach'd his majesty, we standing and observing till they had done; then rising, they led us to the room where the king was. . . .

According to promise, we attended his majesty with samples of our goods, and made our agreements about the prices, tho' not without much difficulty; he and his cappasheirs exacted very high, but at length we concluded as per the latter end. . . .

Capt. Clay and I had agreed to go to the trunk [underground dungeon] to buy the slaves by turns, each his day, that we might have no distraction or disagreement in our trade, as often happens when there are here more ships than one, and the commanders can't set their horses together, and go hand in hand in their traffic, whereby they have a check upon the blacks, whereas their disagreements create animosities, underminings, and out-bidding each other, whereby they enhance the prices to their general loss and detriment, the blacks well knowing how to make the best use of such opportunities, and as we found make it their business, and endeavor to create and foment misunderstandings and jealousies between commanders, it turning to their great account in the disposal of their slaves.

When we were at the trunk, the king's slaves, if he had any, were the first offer'd to sale, which the cappasheirs would be very urgent with us to buy, and would in a manner force us to it ere they would shew us any other, saying they were the *Reys Cosa* [king's slaves], and we must not refuse them, tho' as I observ'd they were generally the worst slaves in the trunk, and we paid more for them than any others, which we could not remedy, it being one of his majesty's prerogatives. Then the cappasheirs each brought out his slaves according to his degree and quality, the greatest first, etc., and our surgeon examin'd them well in all kinds, to see that they were sound wind and limb, making them jump, stretch out their arms swiftly, looking in their mouths to judge of their age; for the cappasheirs are so cunning, that they shave them all close before we see them, so that let them be never be so old we can see no grey hairs in their heads or beards; and then having liquor'd them well and sleek with palm oil, 'tis no easy matter to know an old one from a middle-age one, but by the teeths decay; but our greatest care of all is to buy none that are pox'd, lest they should infect the rest aboard. . . . When we had selected from the rest such as we liked, we agreed in what goods to pay for them, the prices being already stated before the king, how much of each sort of merchandize we were to give for a man, woman, and child, which gave us much ease, and saved abundance of disputes and wranglings, and gave the owner a note, signifying our agreement of the sorts of goods; upon delivery of which the next day he receiv'd them; then we mark'd the slaves we had bought on the breast, or shoulder, with a hot iron, having the letter of the ship's name on it, the place being before anointed with a little palm oil, which caus'd but little pain, the mark being usually well in four or five days, appearing very plain and white after.

DOCUMENT 3.3 | WILLEM BOSMAN, *A New and Accurate Description of the Coast of Guinea* (1703)

In 1637 the Dutch wrested the slave-trading fort at Elmina (present-day Guinea) from the Portuguese. It became the base of operations for the expanding Dutch empire. In his account, Willem Bosman, who served as head of the trading fort, discussed what happened to the slaves between their time of capture and their forced voyage across the Atlantic.

When these slaves come to Fida [the Elmina fort], they are put in prison all together, and when we treat concerning buying them, they are all brought out together in a large plain; where, by our surgeons, whose province it is, they are thoroughly examined, even to the smallest member, and that naked too both men and women, without the least distinction or modesty. . . .

The invalids and the maimed being thrown out, as I have told you, the remainder are numbered, and it is entered who delivered them. In the meanwhile, a burning iron, with the arms or name of the companies, lies in the fire, with which ours are marked on the breast.

This is done that we may distinguish them from the slaves of the English, French, or others (which are also marked with their mark), and to prevent the Negroes exchanging them for worse, at which they have a good hand.

I doubt not but that this trade seems very barbarous to you, but since it is followed by mere necessity, it must go on; but we yet take all possible care that they are not burned too hard, especially the women, who are more tender than the men.

We are seldom long detained in the buying of these slaves, because their price is established, the women being one fourth or fifth part cheaper than the men. The disputes which we generally have with the owners of these slaves are,

Source: Willem Bosman, *A New and Accurate Description of the Coast of Guinea, Divided into the Gold, the Slave, and the Ivory Coasts* (London: J. Knapton, 1705), 364–65.

that we will not give them such goods as they ask for them, especially the boesies [shells] (as I have told you, the money of this country) of which they are very fond, though we generally make a division on this head, in order to make one sort of goods help off another, because those slaves which are paid for in boesies cost the company one half more than those bought with other goods. . . .

When we have agreed with the owners of the slaves, they are returned to their prison; where, from that time forwards, they are kept at our charge, cost us two pence a day a slave; which serves to subsist them, like our criminals, on bread and water: so that to save charges, we send them on board our ships with the very first opportunity, before which their masters strip them of all they have on their backs; so that they come aboard stark naked, as well women as men: in which condition they are obliged to continue, if the master of the ship is not so charitable (which he commonly is) as to bestow something on them to cover their nakedness.

DOCUMENT 3.4 | OLAUDAH EQUIANO, *The Interesting Narrative of the Life of Olaudah Equiano* (1789)

In 1789 Olaudah Equiano published his memoir, one of the first and most important firsthand accounts of slavery. According to his story, he was captured at age eleven, sold into slavery in Barbados, and then sent to Virginia. He later served in the British navy before purchasing his freedom in 1766. In the following excerpt, he describes the horror of the Middle Passage. Recent scholars, however, suggest that Equiano never made the voyage across the Atlantic and may have been born a slave in South Carolina.

At last, when the ship we were in had got in all her cargo, they made ready with many fearful noises, and we were all put under deck, so that we could not see how they managed the vessel. But this disappointment was the least of my sorrow. The stench of the hold while we were on the coast was so intolerably loathsome, that it was dangerous to remain there for any time, and some of us had been permitted to stay on the deck for the fresh air; but now that the whole ship's cargo were confined together, it became absolutely pestilential. The closeness of the place, and the heat of the climate, added to the number in the ship, which was so crowded that each had scarcely room to turn himself, almost suffocated us. This produced copious perspirations, so that the air soon became unfit for respiration, from a variety of loathsome smells, and brought on a sickness among the slaves, of which many died, thus falling victims to the improvident avarice, as I may call it, of their purchasers. This wretched situation was again aggravated by the galling of the chains, now become insupportable, and the filth of the necessary tubs [latrines], into which the children often fell, and were almost

Source: Olaudah Equiano, *The Interesting Narrative of the Life of Olaudah Equiano, Written by Himself* (Boston: Bedford/St. Martins, 2007), 66–68.

suffocated. The shrieks of the women, and the groans of the dying, rendered the whole a scene of horror almost inconceivable. Happily perhaps, for myself, I was soon reduced so low here that it was thought necessary to keep me almost always on deck; and from my extreme youth I was not put in fetters. In this situation I expected every hour to share the fate of my companions, some of whom were almost daily brought upon deck at the point of death, which I began to hope would soon put an end to my miseries. Often did I think many of the inhabitants of the deep much more happy than myself. I envied them the freedom they enjoyed, and as often wished I could change my condition for theirs. Every circumstance I met with served only to render my state more painful, and heighten my apprehensions, and my opinion of the cruelty of the whites. One day they had taken a number of fishes; and when they had killed and satisfied themselves with as many as they thought fit, to our astonishment who were on the deck, rather than give any of them to us to eat, as we expected, they tossed the remaining fish into the sea again, although we begged and prayed for some as well as we could, but in vain; and some of my countrymen, being pressed by hunger, took an opportunity, when they thought no one saw them, of trying to get a little privately; but they were discovered, and the attempt procured them some very severe floggings. One day, when we had a smooth sea and moderate wind, two of my wearied countrymen who were chained together (I was near them at the time), preferring death to such a life of misery, somehow made through the nettings and jumped into the sea; immediately, another quite dejected fellow, who, on account of his illness, was suffered to be out of irons, also followed their example; and I believe many more would very soon have done the same if they had not been prevented by the ship's crew, who were instantly alarmed. Those of us that were the most active were in a moment put down under the deck, and there was such a noise and confusion amongst the people of the ship as I never heard before, to stop her, and get the boat out to go after the slaves. However, two of the wretches were drowned, but they got the other, and afterwards flogged him unmercifully for thus attempting to prefer death to slavery. In this manner we continued to undergo more hardships than I can now relate, hardships which are inseparable from this accursed trade. Many a time we were near suffocation from the want of fresh air, which we were often without for whole days together. This, and the stench of the necessary tubs, carried off many.

INTERPRET THE EVIDENCE

1. What circumstances led to Venture Smith's capture and sale into slavery (Document 3.1)? Who captured and sold him? What does his story reveal about political and military conflict among Africans?

2. With whom did Thomas Phillips have to negotiate to purchase slaves (Document 3.2)? How did he also have to negotiate African political and cultural norms? How does he characterize the slaves he observed?

3. According to Willem Bosman, what happened to slaves in the immediate aftermath of their purchase (Document 3.3)? How did the Dutch analyze and treat their slaves? Why was the branding significant?

4. How did Olaudah Equiano describe his voyage on a slave ship (Document 3.4)? How were the slaves treated? How did they try to resist this treatment?

5. Does the fact that Equiano's narrative may not reflect his actual experience change its value as a historical document? If he did not make the voyage himself, how do you think he described it in such detail? How does this controversy reflect larger issues in studying early American history?

PUT IT IN CONTEXT

1. How did participation in the slave trade shape the history and culture of the British and the Dutch colonies in North America? How might the slave trade have contributed to the development of an African American culture out of the many different groups of Africans brought to the Americas?

DOCUMENT PROJECT

A New Commercial Culture in Boston

The first half of the eighteenth century ushered in dramatic change across the colonies. The population increased fivefold, a demographic shift that squeezed access to land and jobs and increased the numbers of the poor. Yet not all Americans suffered. Many merchants living in northern seaports, for example, accrued unprecedented wealth by participating in an increasingly global trade of goods. In Boston, a new merchant class emerged. Its members built and purchased elaborate homes and decorated them with expensive imported furniture and commissioned family portraits. As a result, the differences between the city's rich and its poor became more visible. Although a broad spectrum of Bostonians participated on some level in the market economy, those who could afford little beyond the necessities of food and clothing resented the conspicuous consumption and increasing political influence of wealthy merchants. The rise of commerce also changed Boston's culture in another significant way: It whittled away the once-dominant influence of religion in the city. Much to the chagrin of Puritan ministers such as Samuel Sewell, it appeared that money had triumphed over piety in New England.

The following documents shed light on the rising commercial culture of Boston during the eighteenth century. As you read, consider the ways in which the buying and selling of goods transformed colonial society. Who played key roles in this process, and who was left out?

DOCUMENT 4.1 | *Ship Arrivals and Departures at Boston* (1707)

As Boston grew in size and its commercial economy expanded, the city became a central hub of international trade. Newspapers kept records of the ships entering and leaving Boston harbor. The following list from a June 1707 edition of the *Boston News-Letter* records arrivals and departures to and from the busy seaport.

Boston	Entered Inward	From
John Bradick	Sloop John & Mary	New York
Abraham Schellinx	Sloop Endeavour	Ditto

Source: *Boston News-Letter*, June 16–June 23, 1707.

Boston	Entered Inward	From
Clemens Sumner	Sloop Speedwell	Connecticut
Walter Reves	Sloop Tryall	Ditto
Joseph Concklin	Sloop Tryall	Ditto
Jeremiah Vaile	Sloop Mary	N. Carolina
John Ruggels	Brigt. Good Luck	Barbadoes
James Barnes	Sloop Endeavour	Antigua
Daniel Noyes	Brigt. Hannover	Hundoras
Jonathan Armitage	Ship Adventure	Ditto
John Price	Brigt. Willi & Mary	Newfoundland

Cleared Outward		For
David Notrhby	Brigt. Speedwell	N. Carolina
James Blin	Sloop Goodhope	Ditto
Dirick Adolph	Sloop Two Brothers	New York
John Rayner	Katch Freek	Newfoundland
Eleazar Johnson	Brigt. Hopewell	Ditto
William Thomas	Brigt. Eagle	Fyall.

Outward Bound		For
John Blower	Ship Stanier Galley	Oporto
Indigo Potter	Sloop Two Brothers	Pensylvania
Lewis Hunt	Sloop Nonsuch	Newfoundland

DOCUMENT 4.2 | *Goods for Sale* (1720)

Merchants used newspapers to advertise their businesses and their wares. The following advertisement displays the diverse merchandise one Boston merchant offered for sale in early 1720. The prices are listed in pounds and shillings, and many of the abbreviations refer to units of measurement such as hogsheads and quintals.

A Catalogue of Sundry Merchandize, with the Prices annexed thereunto

Woolens, Linens, Copper, Brass, and all other European Goods, 200 per Ct. if well bought.

Cotton Wool, 2s. per P. and scarce.

Hollands Duck, 9l. to 9l. 10s. per Piece, & scarce.

Rum N. Eng. 4s. 6d. to 4s. 9d.

English ditto, 7l. 10s. and scarce.

Ditto Barbadoes, 5s.

Madera Wines, None.

Melasses, 2s. to 2s. 4d.

Fiall ditto 20l. per Dipe and scarce.

German Duck broad, None.

Ditto narrow, None.

Swedish Iron, 56l. p. T.

Spanish ditto, 58l. to 60l.

Holland Pots, 56l. per Tun.

English ditto, 50l.

Powder, 11l. per Barrel.

Cordage, 80 to 85s. per C.

Jambee Pepper, 3s. per Pou.

Cheshire Cheese, 12d.

Ditto R. Island, 6d.

Coals, 5l. per Chaldron

Pitch 11s. per C.

Tar, 22s. per Barrel.

Turpentine, 12s. per C.

Oyl Train, 36l. per T. & falling.

Fish Merchantable, 22s. 6d. per Quintal.

Ditto Jamaica, 17s. 6d.

Ditto Barbadoes, 14s. 6d.

Mackeril, None.

Logwood, None.

Barbadoes and other Caribee Sugars, 36 to 60s. per C. and falling.

Cocoa, 7l. per C.

Indigo Jamaica, etc. 8s. to 9s. per Pound.

Rice, None.

Beaver Skins, 3s. 10d.

French and Lisbon Salt, 20s. per Hogs.

Isle of May, etc. 24s.

Buck and Doeskins in Oyl, 8s. 6d. per Pound.

Ditto Ind. Dress, 4s. 6d. to 5s.

Bees Wax, 2s. 2d. per P.

Ditto Bayberry, 16d.

Hops, 4d. per Pound.

Pine Boards, 57s. 6d per Th.

Shingles, 14s.

Pipe Staves, 5 to 8l.

Hogshead Staves Red Oak, 45 to 50s.

Ditto Barrel White Oak, 50s.

Flower, 28s. per C.

Bread Course, 24 to 25s.

Wheat Virginia, 7s. 6d.

Indian Corn, 4s.

Hay, 4s. 6d. per C.

Butter, 11d.

Beef, 3d. half peny.

Pork, 4d. half peny, & falling.

Fraight to London, 50s. per Tun, and 55s. for Turpentine.

DOCUMENT 4.3 | *Advertisement for Musical Instruments* (1716)

Bostonians bought more than just household items and foodstuffs. The following 1716 advertisement reveals the growing market for cultural products in the city.

Advertisements

This is to give notice that there is lately sent over from London a choice collection of musical instruments, consisting of flaguelets, flutes, haut-boys, bas-viols, violins, bows, strings, reeds for haut-boys, books of instructions for all these instruments, books of ruled paper. To be sold at the dancing school of Mr. Enstone in Sudbury-Street near the Orange-Tree Boston. Note, any person may have all instruments of music mended, or virgenalls and spinnets strung and tuned at a reasonable rate, and likewise may be taught to play on any of these instruments abovementioned; dancing taught by a true and easier method than has been heretofore.

Source: *Boston News-Letter*, April 16–April 23, 1716.

DOCUMENT 4.4 | *Chest of Drawers* (c. 1735–1739)

For the colonial elite, home furnishings grew more elaborate—and more expensive—during the eighteenth century. Robert Davis of Boston constructed and decorated this chest of drawers during the 1730s. It represents the "japanned" style of furniture making, in which European and American furniture makers imitated Asian lacquerwork. Colonial Boston became a major center of the japanning trade in America.

DOCUMENT 4.5 | *Advertisement for Runaway Slave* (1744)

Colonial consumption also involved the buying and selling of slaves. Slavery persisted in the North, and slave owners purchased advertisements in newspapers to attempt to retrieve runaways. The following runaway slave advertisement appeared in the July 9, 1744, edition of the *Boston Post-Boy*.

Ran-away again from Mrs. Eleanor Pullen of Boston, on Monday and the 2nd instance, a Negro Woman named Cuba, about 36 Years of Age, a well-fed Wench: She has a Scar over one of her Eye-brows, has lost some of her fore Teeth, speaks good English: She had on when she went away a new cotton linen Shift, a quilted Coat, and a Calico Apron: Whosoever shall take up said Negro and bring her to said Mistress in Com-Court near Fanueil-Hall, shall have Twenty Shillings old Tenor, and all necessary Charges paid.

N.B. All persons are hereby notified not to entertain or harbor said Wench, as they would avoid the Penalty of the law in that Case.

Source: *Boston Post-Boy*, July 9, 1744.

DOCUMENT 4.6 | *Letter from a Boston Protester* (1737)

Many Bostonians resented the increasing power of the merchant class. In 1737 the city, with the support of leading merchants, announced a new public market. In order to sell goods at the new market, farmers and merchants would have to pay a fee. Small farmers and merchants resisted, and many Boston residents decried the new market, asserting that it would lessen competition and increase prices. In response, a group of Bostonians destroyed the new marketplace. Although they offered a handsome reward, police found no witnesses to the crime. The following letter was written anonymously to Boston sheriff Edward Winslow in response to the governor's threat to bring in nearby militia companies to find the perpetrators.

Boston, March 26, 1737

I now in the behalf of myself and others who assembled as a mob assure you, that we have done what we think proper; and are of the opinion, that you had as goods be still and silent, and let alone your drums and guns, for we had no design to do the town any damage, but a great deal of good; and I can assure, that we have above five hundred men in solemn league and covenant to stand by one another, and can procure above seven hundred more of the same mind; so that it will not signify any thing for you with three or four companies of men in arms to suppress us, provided we have not done what we intended; for we are so resolute, that had we any thing further to do, we would do it, provided you loaded your guns with powder and ball; for by the God that made you, if you

Source: *Boston News-Letter*, April 14–April 21, 1737.

come to that, we will find as much powder and ball as you can; so that we will go to a greater length than clubs and staffs: depend upon it that it will be so, as true as there is a God in heaven: Nay, even if you or any of the authority pretend to take the advantage of any man that you or any of you find out was there, we will resent it and cause you and the whole authority to repent of any such proceeding: So I beg and pray that the Lord of heaven and earth will keep you from taking any advantage upon any man; for I do now declare in the name of 500 men, that it will be the hardest place of work that ever you took in hand, to pretend to commit any man for that night's work, or at least keep them when committed; so that Governour Belcher himself may pretend to do what he will, there must be a great deal of blood shed before we will be suppressed, provided you take any advantage of us or any of us.

From your unknown friend and servant, Blank

INTERPRET THE EVIDENCE

1. According to the 1707 entries and clearances list, what was the scope of the trade that came through Boston by the early eighteenth century (Document 4.1)? How might Boston have become such an international center of commerce?

2. What items did the Boston merchant advertise for sale (Document 4.2)? Where did the items come from? Why do you think he advertised many of his products by their place of origin? Who do you think was the market for these items?

3. What services does the merchant selling musical instruments offer (Document 4.3)? How does he describe his prices? What Bostonians do you think were interested in these items?

4. Describe the chest of drawers made and decorated by Robert Davis (Document 4.4). What functions does it serve? Why do you think the owner purchased this piece of furniture?

5. How does the *Boston Post-Boy* advertisement describe the runaway slave (Document 4.5)? What does the ad reveal about owner Eleanor Pullen's knowledge of the slave Cuba? What rewards and threats does Pullen offer to ensure the return of Cuba?

6. How does the protest letter defend the destruction of the market (Document 4.6)? What do the authors say will happen if the governor brings in militia? How would you characterize the author's rhetoric? Why do you think nobody came forward as a witness to the crime?

PUT IT IN CONTEXT

1. How did the commercial culture of Boston accentuate class differences in the early eighteenth century? How might it have brought people together within particular classes or across class lines?

Defining Liberty, Defining America

With the failure of the Albany Plan of Union in 1754, it appeared the colonies would not soon unite under a common government. But the conflicts of the 1760s and 1770s prompted many colonists to ask questions about the meaning of liberty under the British crown. The acts and duties imposed by Parliament angered colonists, who believed they had little say in the decision-making process. They resisted in a number of ways, including nonimportation agreements, boycotts, and petitions. At the same time, the colonists had to figure out how to forge new ties among themselves. Broad-based protests would work only if far-flung Americans could communicate effectively. Anger toward Parliament led colonists to band together in resistance.

Discussions over the meanings of liberty and the increasing interconnectedness of the colonies in political matters led many to wonder about the specific qualities of being an American. Most commentators stressed liberty. Yet this liberty applied primarily to whites only, as free and enslaved blacks as well as Indians rarely had the same opportunities.

The following documents examine the evolution of this process—of thirteen colonies increasingly coming to see themselves as part of a larger political entity, even though the idea of declaring independence remained unpopular until the eve of the Revolution. As you read, think about how and why historical circumstances changed so dramatically between 1754 and 1773.

DOCUMENT 5.1 | *The Albany Plan of Union* (1754)

When British leaders called a meeting of colonists and Iroquois Indians in Albany in June 1754, Benjamin Franklin seized the opportunity to present his plan for a council of colonial representatives. His Plan of Union details the Albany Congress's proposals regarding defense, Indian policies, trade, and the mechanics of government. Although both the British and the majority of the colonists rejected the document, it did signal that some colonial leaders had begun to think about new forms of representation within the British empire.

Source: William MacDonald, ed., *Select Charters and Other Documents Illustrative of American History, 1606–1775* (New York: The MacMillan Company, 1906), 254–57.

PLAN of a proposed UNION of the several Colonies of Massachusetts Bay, New Hampshire, Connecticut, Rhode Island, New York, New Jerseys, Pennsylvania, Maryland, Virginia, North Carolina, and South Carolina, for their mutual defence and security, and for extending the British Settlements in North America.

That humble application be made for an Act of the Parliament of Great Brittain, by virtue of which, one General Government may be formed in America, including all the said Colonies, within, and under which Government each Colony may retain its present constitution, except in the particulars wherein a charge [*change*] may be directed by the said Act, as hereafter follows.

That the said General Government be administered by a president General, to be appointed & supported by the Crown, and a grand Council to be chosen by the representatives of the people of the several Colonies, meet[ing] in their respective assemblies.

That within Months after the passing of such Act, The house of representatives in the several Assemblies, that Happen to be sitting within that time or that shall be specially for that purpose convened, may and shall chose, Members for the Grand Council in the following proportions, that is to say:

Massachusetts Bay	7.
New Hampshire	2.
Connecticut	5.
Rhode Island	2.
New York	4.
New Jerseys	3.
Pennsylvania	6.
Maryland	4.
Virginia	7.
North Carolina	4.
South Carolina	4.
	48.

Who shall meet for the present time at the City of Philadelphia in Pennsylvania, being called by the President General as soon as conveniently may be after his appointment.

That there shall be a New Election of the Members of the Grand Council every three years, and on the death or resignation of any Member, his place should be supplyed by a new choice at the next sitting of the Assembly of the Colony he represented.

That after the first three years, when the proportion of money arising out of each Colony to the General Treasury can be known, the number of Members to be chosen, for each Colony shall from time to time in all ensuing Elections be regulated by that proportion (yet so as that the Number to be chosen by any one province be not more than seven nor less than two).

That the Grand Council shall meet once in every year, and oftener if occasion require, at such time and place as they shall adjourn to at the last preceeding meeting, or as they shall be called to meet at by the President General, on any emergency, he having first obtained in writing the consent of seven of the Members to such call, and sent due and timely notice to the whole.

That the Grand Council have power to chuse their speaker, and shall neither be dissolved prorogued, nor continue sitting longer than six weeks at one time without their own consent, or the special command of the Crown.

That the Members of the Grand Council shall be allowed for their service ten shillings sterling per diem, during their Sessions or [*and*] Journey to and from the place of Meeting; twenty miles to be reckoned a days Journey.

That the Assent of the President General be requisite to all Acts of the Grand Council, and that it be his Office and duty to cause them to be carried into execution.

That the President General with the advice of the Grand Council, hold or direct all Indian Treaties in which the general interest of the Colonys may be concerned; and make peace or declare War with Indian Nations. That they make such Laws as they judge necessary for the regulating all Indian Trade. That they make all purchases from Indians for the Crown, of lands not [now] within the bounds of particular Colonies, or that shall not be within their bounds when some of them are reduced to more convenient dimensions. That they make new settlements on such purchases by granting Lands, [in the King's name] reserving a Quit rent to the Crown, for the use of the General Treasury.

That they make Laws for regulating & governing such new settlements, till the Crown shall think fit to form them into particular Governments.

That they raise and pay Soldiers, and build Forts for the defence of any of the Colonies, and equip vessels of Force to guard the Coasts and protect the Trade on the Ocean, Lakes, or great Rivers; but they shall not impress men in any Colonies without the consent of its Legislature. That for these purposes they have power to make Laws and lay and Levy such general duties, imposts or taxes, as to them shall appear most equal and just, considering the ability and other circumstances of the Inhabitants in the several Colonies, and such as may be collected with the least inconvenience to the people, rather discouraging luxury, than loading Industry with unnecessary burthens. — That they might appoint a General Treasurer and a particular Treasurer in each Government when necessary, and from time to time may order the sums in the Treasuries of each Government, into the General Treasury, or draw on them for special payments as they find most convenient; yet no money to issue but by joint orders of the President General and Grand Council, except where sums have been appropriated to particular purposes, and the President General is previously impowered by an Act to draw for such sums.

That the General accounts shall be yearly settled and reported to the several Assemblies.

That a Quorum of the Grand Council impowered to act with the President General, do consist of twenty five Members, among whom there shall be one or more from a majority of the Colonies. That the laws made by them for the purposes aforesaid, shall not be repugnant, but as near as may be agreeable to the Laws of England, and shall be transmitted to the King in Council for approbation, as soon as may be after their passing, and if not disapproved within three years after presentation to remain in Force.

That in case of the death of the President General, the Speaker of the Grand Council for the time being shall succeed, and be vested with the same powers and authority, to continue until the King's pleasure be known.

That all Military Commission Officers, whether for land or sea service, to act under this General constitution, shall be nominated by the President General, but the aprobation of the Grand Council is to be obtained before they receive their Commissions; and all Civil Officers are to be nominated by the Grand Council, and to receive the President General's approbation before the officiate; but in case of vacancy by death or removal of any Officer Civil or Military under this constitution, The Governor of the Province in which such vacancy happens, may appoint till the pleasure of the President General and Grand Council can be known. — That the particular Military as well as Civil establishments in each Colony remain in their present State this General constitution notwithstanding. And that on sudden emergencies any Colony may defend itself, and lay the accounts of expence thence arisen, before the President General and Grand Council, who may allow and order payment of the same as far as they judge such accounts just and reasonable.

DOCUMENT 5.2 | *Boycott Agreement of Women in Boston* (1770)

By 1770 the political climate had changed in the American colonies. The passage of the Sugar, Stamp, and Townshend Acts had inflamed tensions between the colonists and the crown. Protests increased, and these protests opened the door for women to participate informally in politics. The following document is an agreement signed by more than three hundred women in Boston.

The following Agreement has lately been come into by upwards of 300 Mistresses of Families in this Town; in which Number the Ladies of the highest Rank and Influence, that could be waited upon in so short a Time, are included.

Boston, January 31, 1770

At a time when our invaluable Rights and Privileges are attacked in an unconstitutional and most alarming Manner, and as we find we are reproached for not being so ready as could be desired, to lend our Assistance, we think it our Duty perfectly to concur with the true Friends of Liberty, in all the Measures they have taken to save this abused Country from Ruin and Slavery: And particularly, we join with the very respectable Body of Merchants, and other Inhabitants of this Town, who met in Faneuil-Hall the 23rd of this Instant, in their Resolutions, *totally* to abstain from the Use of TEA: And as the greatest Part of the Revenue arising by Virtue of the late Acts, is produced from the Duty

Source: *Boston Evening-Post*, February 12, 1770.

paid upon Tea, which Revenue is wholly expended to support the American Board of Commissioners, We the Subscribers do strictly engage, that we will *totally* abstain from the Use of that Article (Sickness excepted) not only in our respective Families; but that we will absolutely refuse it, if it should be offered to us upon any Occasion whatsoever. This agreement we cheerfully come into, as we believe the very distressed Situation of our Country requires it, and we do hereby oblige ourselves religiously to observe it, till the late Revenue Acts are repealed.

DOCUMENT 5.3 | PETER BESTES AND MASSACHUSETTS SLAVES, *Letter to Local Representatives* (1773)

The rhetoric of freedom resonated with slaves, who sought to make a case for their own liberty. In 1773 Peter Bestes and other slaves in Massachusetts sent the following letter to local officials. It was subsequently published as a broadside and distributed throughout Massachusetts.

BOSTON, April 20th, 1773

SIR,

THE efforts made by the legislative of this province in their last sessions to free themselves from slavery, gave us, who are in that deplorable state, a high degree of satisfaction. We expect great things from men who have made such a noble stand against the designs of their *fellow-men* to enslave them. We cannot but wish and hope Sir, that you will have the same grand object, we mean civil and religious liberty, in view in your next session. The divine spirit of *freedom*, seems to fire every humane breast on this continent, except such as are bribed to assist in executing the execrable plan.

WE are very sensible that it would be highly detrimental to our present masters, if we were allowed to demand all that of *right* belongs to us for past services; this we disclaim. Even the *Spaniards*, who have not those sublime ideas of freedom that English men have, are conscious that they have no right to all the services of their fellow-men, we mean the *Africans*, whom they have purchased with their money; therefore they allow them one day in a week to work for themselve[s], to enable them to earn money to purchase the residue of their time, which they have a right to demand in such portions as they are able to pay for (a due appraizment of their services being first made, which always stands at the purchase money). We do not pretend to dictate to you Sir, or to the honorable Assembly, of which you are a member: We acknowledge our obligations to you for what you have already done, but as the people of this province seem to be actuated by the principles of equity and justice, we cannot but expect your house

Source: Woody Holton, *Black Americans in the Revolutionary Era: A Brief History with Documents* (Boston: Bedford/St. Martin's, 2009), 46–47.

will again take our deplorable case into serious consideration, and give us that ample relief which, *as men*, we have a natural right to.

BUT since the wise and righteous governor of the universe, has permitted our fellow men to make us slaves, we bow in submission to him, and determine to behave in such a manner, as that we may have reason to expect the divine approbation of, and assistance in, our peaceable and lawful attempts to gain our freedom.

WE are willing to submit to such regulations and laws, as may be made relative to us, until we leave the province, which we determine to do as soon as we can from our joynt labours procure money to transport ourselves to some part of the coast of *Africa*, where we propose a settlement. We are very desirous that you should have instructions relative to us, from your town, therefore we pray you to communicate this letter to them, and ask this favor for us.

In behalf of our fellow slaves in this province,

And by order of their Committee.
PETER BESTES,
SAMBO FREEMAN,
FELIX HOLBROOK,
CHESTER JOIE.

DOCUMENT 5.4 | *Committees of Correspondence* (1773)

The first committee of correspondence formed in Massachusetts in the wake of the Sugar Act. While the original group was ineffective, additional, more successful committees of correspondence organized to communicate information throughout the colonies and to coordinate protests during the 1770s. The Boston committee of correspondence circulated this letter from the Virginia committee in April 1773.

BOSTON, APRIL 9, 1773.

SIR,

THE Committee of Correspondence of this Town have received the following Intelligence, communicated to them by a Person of Character in this Place. We congratulate you upon the Acquisition of such respectable Aid as the ancient and patriotic Province of *Virginia*, the earliest Resolvers against the detestable Stamp-Act, in Opposition to the unconstitutional Measures of the present Administration. The Authenticity of this Advice you may depend upon, as it was immediately received from one of the Honorable Gentlemen appointed to communicate with the other Colonies.

We are,

Your Friends and humble Servants,

Source: Printed Broadside from Massachusetts Historical Society, Boston, 1773.

Signed by Direction of the Committee for Correspondence in *Boston*, William Cooper Town-Clerk.

To the Town-Clerk of [blank], to be immediately delivered to the Committee of Correspondence for your Town, if such a Committee is chosen, otherwise to the Gentlemen the Selectmen, to be communicated to the Town.

Extract of a Letter from a Gentleman of distinction in Virginia, to his Friend in this Town, dated March 14th, 1773.

"I RECEIVED the papers you sent me, and am much obliged to you for them, our assembly sitting a few days after, they were of use to us. You will see by the enclosed Resolutions the true sentiments of this colony, and that we are endeavouring to bring our sister colonies into the strictest union with us, that we may RESENT IN ONE BODY any steps that may be taken by administration to deprive ANY ONE OF US of the least particle of our rights & liberties; we should have done more but we could procure nothing but news-paper accounts of the proceedings in Rhode-Island. I hope we shall not be thus kept in the dark for the future, and that we shall have from the different Committees the earliest intelligence of any motion that may be made by the TYRANTS in England to carry their INFERNAL purposes of enslaving us into execution; I dare venture to assure you the strictest attention will be given on our parts to these grand points."

In the House *of* Burgesses, in *Virginia March*, 1773.

"WHEREAS the minds of his Majesty's faithful subjects in this colony have been much disturbed by various rumours and reports of proceedings tending to deprive them of their ancient, legal and constitutional rights.

"And whereas the affairs of this colony are frequently connected with those of Great Britain, as well as of the neighbouring colonies, which renders a communication of sentiments necessary, in order therefore to remove the uneasinesses and to quiet the minds of the people, as well as for the other good purposes above mentioned.

"Be it *resolved*, That a standing committee of correspondence and inquiry be appointed, to consist of eleven persons, viz. the honourable Payton Randolph, Esq; Robert Carter Nicholas, Richard Bland, Richard Henry Lee, Benjamin Harrison, Edmund Pendleton, Patrick Henry, Dudley Digges, Dabney Carr, Archibald Cary, and Thomas Jefferson, Esqrs; any six of whom to be a committee, whose business it shall be to obtain the most early and authentic intelligence of all such acts and resolutions of the British parliament or proceedings of administration, as may relate to, or affect the British colonies in America, and to keep up and maintain a correspondence and communication with our sister colonies, respecting these important considerations, and the result of such their proceedings from time to time to lay before this house.

"*Resolved,* That it be an instruction to the said committee, that they do, without delay, inform themselves particularly of the principles and authority, on which was constituted a court of inquiry, said to have been lately held in Rhode-Island, with powers to transport persons accused of offences committed in America, to places beyond the seas to be tried.

"*Resolved,* That the Speaker of this House do transmit to the Speakers of the different assemblies of the British colonies, on this continent, copies of the said resolutions, and desire they will lay them before their respective assemblies, and request them to appoint some person or persons of their respective bodies, to communicate from time to time with the said committee."

DOCUMENT 5.5 | J. HECTOR ST. JOHN DE CREVECOEUR, *Letters from an American Farmer* (1782)

As the debates over liberty and the relationship between the colonies crested in the 1770s, J. Hector St. John de Crevecoeur asked the question, "What is an American?" A former French militia officer, Crevecoeur had moved to New York in 1759. In 1782 he published *Letters from an American Farmer*, the culmination of a manuscript he had been working on during the previous decade. In the following excerpts, Crevecoeur attempts to answer the question of what makes an American and outlines his thoughts on slavery after a visit to Charles Town (later Charleston), South Carolina.

He is arrived on a new continent; a modern society offers itself to his contemplation, different from what he had hitherto seen. It is not composed, as in Europe, of great lords who possess every thing, and of a herd of people who have nothing. Here are no aristocratical families, no courts, no kings, no bishops, no ecclesiastical dominion, no invisible power giving to a few a very visible one; no great manufacturers employing thousands, no great refinements of luxury. The rich and the poor are not so far removed from each other as they are in Europe. Some few towns excepted, we are all tillers of the earth, from Nova Scotia to West Florida. We are a people of cultivators, scattered over an immense territory, communicating with each other by means of good roads and navigable rivers, united by the silken bands of mild government, all respecting the laws, without dreading their power, because they are equitable. We are all animated with the spirit of an industry which is unfettered and unrestrained, because each person works for himself. If he travels through our rural districts he views not the hostile castle, and the haughty mansion, contrasted with the clay-built hut and miserable cabbin, where cattle and men help to keep each other warm, and dwell in meanness, smoke, and indigence. A pleasing uniformity of decent competence appears throughout our habitations. The meanest of our log-houses is a dry and comfortable habitation. Lawyer or merchant are the fairest titles our towns afford;

Source: J. Hector St. John de Crevecoeur, *Letters from an American Farmer* (1782; reprint New York: Fox, Duffield & Company, 1904), 49–50, 54–55, 225, 227.

that of a farmer is the only appellation of the rural inhabitants of our country. It must take some time ere he can reconcile himself to our dictionary, which is but short in words of dignity, and names of honour. There, on a Sunday, he sees a congregation of respectable farmers and their wives, all clad in neat homespun, well mounted, or riding in their own humble waggons. There is not among them an esquire, saving the unlettered magistrate. There he sees a parson as simple as his flock, a farmer who does not riot on the labour of others. We have no princes, for whom we toil, starve, and bleed: we are the most perfect society now existing in the world. Here man is free as he ought to be; nor is this pleasing equality so transitory as many others are. . . .

What then is the American, this new man? He is either an European, or the descendant of an European, hence that strange mixture of blood, which you will find in no other country. I could point out to you a family whose grandfather was an Englishman, whose wife was Dutch, whose son married a French woman, and whose present four sons have now four wives of different nations. *He* is an American, who leaving behind him all his ancient prejudices and manners, receives new ones from the new mode of life he has embraced, the new government he obeys, and the new rank he holds. He becomes an American by being received in the broad lap of our great *Alma Mater*. Here individuals of all nations are melted into a new race of men, whose labours and posterity will one day cause great changes in the world. Americans are the western pilgrims, who are carrying along with them that great mass of arts, sciences, vigour, and industry which began long since in the east; they will finish the great circle. The Americans were once scattered all over Europe; here they are incorporated into one of the finest systems of population which has ever appeared, and which will hereafter become distinct by the power of the different climates they inhabit. The American ought therefore to love this country much better than that wherein either he or his forefathers were born. Here the rewards of his industry follow with equal steps the progress of his labour; his labour is founded on the basis of nature, *self-interest*; can it want a stronger allurement? Wives and children, who before in vain demanded of him a morsel of bread, now, fat and frolicsome, gladly help their father to clear those fields whence exuberant crops are to arise to feed and to clothe them all; without any part being claimed, either by a despotic prince, a rich abbot, or a mighty lord. . . .

While all is joy, festivity, and happiness in Charles-Town, would you imagine that scenes of misery overspread in the country? Their ears by habit are become deaf, their hearts are hardened; they neither see, hear, nor feel for the woes of their poor slaves, from whose painful labours all their wealth proceeds. Here the horrors of slavery, the hardship of incessant toils, are unseen; and no one thinks with compassion of those showers of sweat and of tears which from the bodies of Africans, daily drop, and moisten the ground they till. . . .

Strange order of things! Oh, Nature, where art thou?—Are not these blacks thy children as well as we? On the other side, nothing is to be seen but the most diffusive misery and wretchedness, unrelieved even in thought or wish! Day after day they drudge on without any prospect of ever reaping for themselves; they are obliged to devote their lives, their limbs, their will, and every vital exertion to swell the wealth of masters; who look not upon them with half the kindness and affection with which they consider their dogs and horses. Kindness and affection are not the portion of those who till the earth, who carry the burdens, who convert the logs into useful boards. This reward, simple and natural as one would conceive it, would border on humanity; and planters must have none of it!

INTERPRET THE EVIDENCE

1. What powers would the general government have had under the Albany Plan of Union (Document 5.1)? How did it deal with the colonies' relationship to Britain? How did it regulate their relationship with Indians? How much power would individual colonies have had in the general government?

2. What do the women who signed the boycott agreement pledge to do in protest of the Townshend Acts (Document 5.2)? How do they characterize the relationship between the crown and the colonies? How would you describe their rhetoric?

3. What is the basis of Peter Bestes and his fellow slaves' call for freedom (Document 5.3)? What does the letter have to say about the slaves' masters? What do the slaves hope to do once they gain their freedom? How does their rhetoric compare to that of the women in Document 5.2?

4. Why do you think the Boston committee of correspondence circulated this letter (Document 5.4) from Virginia? What did the Virginians propose? What is the significance of the capitalized words in the letter? What does the letter say about the way these colonists perceived the relationship between colonies?

5. What, according to J. Hector St. John de Crevecoeur, is an American (Document 5.5)? Do you think his analysis is romantic or accurate (or perhaps both)? How does slavery fit into his story? Why do you think he called his work *Letters from an American Farmer*?

PUT IT IN CONTEXT

1. How did the authors of these documents describe and invoke the idea of connections among the colonists? Why were these arguments more persuasive in 1773 than in 1754?

6

Loyalists in the American Revolution

On the eve of the American Revolution, perhaps half the colonists favored independence, while roughly one-fifth remained committed to Great Britain. Once the fighting began, those loyalists who fought for the crown faced great scrutiny in the newly independent United States. Still, a great number of Americans refused to renounce Great Britain.

Loyalists made their decision for a number of reasons, some ideological, others more practical. The following documents illuminate not only arguments in favor of remaining loyal to the crown but also the experiences of those who made that choice. Joseph Galloway (Document 6.1) was a delegate to the Continental Congress; his pleas for union and reconciliation reached the ears of the most powerful colonists. Thomas Paine's popular pro-independence pamphlet *Common Sense* inspired rebukes from Reverend Charles Inglis (Document 6.2) and poet Hannah Griffits (Document 6.3). The Mohawk leader Joseph Brant (Document 6.4) and South Carolina slave Boston King (Document 6.5) sided with Great Britain for altogether different reasons. Those loyalists who did not flee to enemy lines were subjected to a number of persuasive tactics to convert them to the patriot cause. In examining these sources, consider which groups of colonists would have been more likely to support the loyalist argument.

DOCUMENT 6.1 | JOSEPH GALLOWAY, *Speech to Continental Congress* (1774)

Joseph Galloway served as a Pennsylvania delegate to the First Continental Congress. He did not support independence and attempted to moderate the increasing tensions between the crown and the colonists. He offered a "Plan of Union" in hopes of giving the colonists more power in Parliament without breaking their ties to Great Britain. On September 28, 1774, Galloway made the following address to the congress. Within two years, he had moved to Britain.

I will therefore call your recollection to the dangerous situation of the Colonies from the intrigues of France, and the incursions of the Canadians and their Indian

Source: *Journals of the Continental Congress, 1774–1789*, vol. 1, 1774 (Washington, D.C.: U.S. Government Printing Office, 1904), 45–47.

allies, at the commencement of the last war. None of us can be ignorant of the just sense they then entertained of that danger, and of their incapacity to defend themselves against it, nor of the supplications made to the Parent State for its assistance, nor of the cheerfulness with which Great-Britain sent over her fleets and armies for their protection, of the millions she expended in that protection, and of the happy consequences which attended it.

In this state of the Colonies it was not unreasonable to expect that Parliament would have levied a tax on them proportionate to their wealth, and the sums raised in Great Britain. Her ancient right, so often exercised, and never contro-verted, enabled her, and the occasion invited her, to do it. And yet, not knowing their wealth, a generous tenderness arising from the fear of doing them injustice, induced Parliament to forbear to levy aids upon them—It left the Colonies to do justice to themselves and to the nation. And moreover, in order to allure them to a discharge of their duty, it offered to reimburse those Colonies which should generously grant the aids that were necessary to their own safety. But what was the conduct of the Colonies on this occasion, in which their own existence was immediately concerned? However painful it may be for me to repeat, or you to hear, I must remind you of it. You all know there were Colonies which at some times granted liberal aids, and at others nothing; other Colonies gave nothing during the war; none gave equitably in proportion to their wealth, and all that did give were actuated by partial and self-interested motives, and gave only in proportion to the approach or remoteness of the danger. These delinquencies were occasioned by the want of the exercise of some supreme power to ascertain, with equity, their proportions of aids, and to over-rule the particular passions, prejudices, and interests, of the several Colonies. . . .

The advocates for the supremacy of Parliament . . . assert, what we cannot deny—That the discovery of the Colonies was made under a commission granted by the supreme authority of the British State, that they have been settled under that authority, and therefore are truly the property of that State. Parliamentary jurisdic-tion has been constantly exercised over them from their first settlement; its execu-tive authority has ever run through all their inferior political systems: the Colonists have ever sworn allegiance to the British State, and have been considered, both by the State and by themselves, as subjects of the British Government. Protection and allegiance are reciprocal duties; the one cannot exist without the other. The Colonies cannot claim the protection of Britain upon any principle of reason or law, while they deny its supreme authority. Upon this ground the authority of Parliament stands too firm to be shaken by any arguments whatever; and therefore to deny that authority, and at the same time to declare their incapacity to be repre-sented, amounts to a full and explicit declaration of independence. . . .

I would therefore acknowledge the necessity of the supreme authority of Parliament over the Colonies, because it is a proposition which we cannot deny without manifest contradiction, while we confess that we are subjects of the Brit-ish Government; and if we do not approve of a representation in Parliament, let us ask for a participation in the freedom and power of the English constitution in some other mode of incorporation: for I am convinced, by long attention to the subject, that let us deliberate, and try what other expedients we may, we shall find none that can give to the Colonies substantial freedom, but some such incorporation. I therefore beseech you, by the respect you are bound to pay to the instructions of your constituents, by the regard you have for the honour and safety of your country, and as you wish to avoid a war with Great-Britain, which must terminate, at all events in the ruin of America, not to rely on a denial of the authority of Parliament, a refusal to be represented, and on a non-importation agreement; because whatever protestations, in that case, may be made to the contrary, it will prove to the world that we intend to throw off our allegiance to the State, and to involve the two countries in all the horrors of a civil war.

DOCUMENT 6.2 | CHARLES INGLIS, *The True Interest of America Impartially Stated* (1776)

Perhaps no other work in American history had the immediate impact of Thomas Paine's *Common Sense*. While it tilted many indecisive colonists to the side of independence, it also alienated those who wanted to remain a part of the British empire. The Reverend Charles Inglis, a British-born Anglican minister living in New York City, offered the following response to Paine's pamphlet.

I think it no difficult matter to point out many advantages which will certainly attend our reconciliation and connection with Great-Britain, on a firm, constitutional plan. I shall select a few of these; and that their importance may be more clearly discerned. . . .

1. By a reconciliation with Britain, a period would be put to the present calamitous war, by which so many lives have been lost, and so many more must be lost, if it continues. This alone is an advantage devoutly to be wished for. This author [Thomas Paine] says—"The blood of the slain, the weeping voice of nature cries, 'Tis time to part." I think they cry just the reverse. The blood of the slain, the weeping voice of nature cries—It is time to be reconciled; it is time to lay aside those animosities which have pushed on Britons to shed the blood of Britons; it is high time that those who are connected by the endearing ties of religion, kindred and country, should resume their former friendship, and be united in the bond of mutual affection, as their interests are inseparably united.

2. By a Reconciliation with Great-Britain, Peace—that fairest offspring and gift of Heaven—will be restored. In one respect Peace is like health; we do not sufficiently know its value but by its absence. What uneasiness and anxiety, what evils has this short interruption of peace with the parent-state brought on the whole British empire! . . .

3. Agriculture, commerce, and industry would resume their wonted vigor. At present they languish and droop, both here and in Britain; and must continue to do so while this unhappy contest remains unsettled.

Source: Charles Inglis, *The True Interest of America Impartially Stated, in Certain Strictures on a Pamphlet Intitled* [sic] *Common Sense* (Philadelphia: James Humphreys, 1776), 47–49.

4. By a connection with Great-Britain, our trade would still have the protection of the greatest naval power in the world. England has the advantage, in this respect, of every other state, whether of ancient or modern times. . . . To suppose, with our author, that we should have no war, were we to revolt from England, is too absurd to deserve a confutation. I could just as soon set about refuting the reveries of some brain-sick enthusiast. Past experience shews that Britain is able to defend our commerce, and our coasts; and we have no reason to doubt of her being able to do so for the future.

5. The protection of our trade, while connected with Britain, will not cost a *fiftieth* part of what it must cost, were we ourselves to raise a naval force sufficient for this purpose.

6. Whilst connected with Great-Britain, we have a bounty on almost every article of exportation; and we may be better supplied with goods by her, than we could elsewhere. What our author says is true—"that our imported goods must be paid for, buy them where we will"; but we may buy them dearer, and of worse quality, in one place than another. The manufactures of Great-Britain confessedly surpass any in the world—particularly those in every kind of metal, which we want most; and no country can afford linens and woollens, of equal quality cheaper.

7. When a Reconciliation is effected, and things return into the old channel, a few years of peace will restore everything to its pristine state. Emigrants will flow in as usual from the different parts of Europe. Population will advance with the same rapid progress as formerly, and our lands will rise in value.

DOCUMENT 6.3 | HANNAH GRIFFITS, *Response to Thomas Paine* (1777)

Just as many women agitated in favor of independence and fought in the war on the patriot side, others argued in favor of reconciliation with Britain. Like Charles Inglis, Hannah Griffits, a Quaker from Philadelphia, took offense to what she viewed as Thomas Paine's extremism. She wrote the following poem in April 1777 in response to "The American Crisis," a series of articles written by Thomas Paine during the Revolutionary War.

On reading a few Paragraphs in the Crisis

April 1777

Paine, tho' thy Tongue may now run glibber,
Warm'd with thy Independent Glow,
Thou art indeed, the boldest Fibber.

Source: David S. Shields, ed., *American Poetry: The Seventeenth and Eighteenth Centuries* (New York: The Library of America, 2007), 562–63.

I ever knew or wish to know.
Here Page & Page, ev'n num'rous Pages,
Are void of Breeding, Sense or Truth,
I hope thou don't receive thy Wages,
As Tutor to our rising Youth.
Of female Manners never scribble,
Nor with thy Rudeness wound our Ear,
How e'er thy trimming Pen may quibble,
The Delicate — is not thy Sphere;
And now to prove how false thy Stories
By Facts, — which wont admit a Doubt
Know there are conscientious Tories
And one poor Whig at least without
Wilt thou permit the Muse to mention,
A Whisper circulated round,
"Let Howe encrease the Scribblers Pension
No more will Paine a Whig be found." —
For not from Principle, but Lucre,
He gains his Bread from out the Fire,
Let Court & Congress, both stand neuter,
And the poor Creature must expire.

DOCUMENT 6.4 | *Joseph Brant (Mohawk) Expresses Loyalty to the Crown* (1776)

The conflict between the colonists and the crown forced American Indians to make difficult choices. For Joseph Brant of the Mohawks, and for most other members of the Iroquois Confederacy, siding with the British forces appeared to be the best option once it became clear that neutrality would not hold. Even as early as 1776, however, Brant recognized that his people were unlikely to receive equal treatment from their British allies.

Brother Gorah,

We have cross'd the great Lake and come to this kingdom with our Superintendent, Col. Johnson, from our Confederacy the Six Nations and their allies, that we might see our Father, the Great King, and joyn in informing him, his Councillors and wise men, of the good intentions of the Indians our brethren, and of their attachment to His Majesty and his Government.

Brother. The Disturbances in America give great trouble to all our Nations, as many strange stories have been told to us by the people of that country. The Six

Source: E. B. O'Callaghan, ed., *Documents Relative to the Colonial History of the State of New York*, 15 vols. (Albany, 1853–1887), 8:670–71.

Nations who always loved the king, sent a number of their Chiefs and Warriors with their Superintendent to Canada last summer, where they engaged their allies to joyn with them in the defense of that country, and when it was invaded by the New England people they alone defeated them.

Brother. In that engagement we had several of our best Warriors killed and wounded, and the Indians think it very hard they should have been so deceived by the White people in that country, the enemy returning in great numbers, and no White people supporting the Indians, they were obliged to return to their villages and sit still. We now Brother hope to see these bad children chastised, and that we may be enabled to tell the Indians who have always been faithfull and ready to assist the King, what his Majesty intends.

Brother. The Mohocks our particular nation, have on all occasions shewn their zeal and loyalty to the Great King; yet they have been very badly treated by the people in that country, the City of Albany laying an unjust claim to the lands on which our Lower Castle is built, as one Klock, and others do to those of Conijoharrie our Upper Village. We have often been assured by our late great friend Sr William Johnson who never deceived us, and we know he was told so that the King and wise men here would do us justice; but this notwithstanding all our applications has never been done, and it makes us very uneasie. We also feel for the distress in which our Brethren on the Susquehanna are likely to be involved by a mistake made in the Boundary we setled in 1768. This also our Superintendent has laid before the King, and we beg it may be remembered. And also concerning Religion and the want of Ministers of the Church of England, he knows the designs of those bad people and informs us he has laid the same before the King. We have only therefore to request that his Majesty will attend to this matter: it troubles our Nation & they can not sleep easie in their beds. Indeed it is very hard when we have let the Kings subjects have so much land for so little value, they should want to cheat us in this manner of the small spots we have left for our women and children to live on. We are tired out in making complaints & getting no redress. We therefore hope that the Assurances now given us by the Superintendent may take place, and that he may have it in his power to procure us justice.

Brother. We shall truly report all that we hear from you, to the Six Nations on our return. We are well informed there have been many Indians in this Country who came without any authority, from their own, and gave us much trouble. We desire Brother to tell you this is not our case. We are warriors known to all the Nations, and are now here by approbation of many of them, whose sentiments we speak.

Brother. We hope these things will be considered and that the King or his great men will give us such an answer as will make our hearts light and glad before we go, and strengthen our hands, so that we may joyn our Superintendent, Col. Johnson in giving satisfaction to all our Nations, when we report to them on our return; for which purpose we hope soon to be accommodated with a passage.

Dictated by the Indians and taken down by Jo. Chew. Secretary

DOCUMENT 6.5 | BOSTON KING, *Memoirs of the Life of Boston King* (1798)

The experiences of the South Carolina slave Boston King dramatize why many slaves sided with the British. King took advantage of the British decision to grant freedom to any slave who escaped and joined the British military effort. After the fighting concluded, he gained his freedom but was required to leave the United States, as he described in his memoir.

My master being apprehensive that Charles Town was in danger on account of the war, removed into the country, about 38 miles off. Here we built a large house for Mr. Waters, during which time the English took Charles Town. Having obtained leave one day to see my parents, who had lived about 12 miles off, and it being late before I could go, I was obliged to borrow one of Mr. Waters's horses; but a servant of my master's took the horse from me to go a little journey, and stayed two or three days longer than he ought. This involved me in the greatest perplexity, and I expected the severest punishment, because the gentleman to whom the horse belonged was a very bad man, and knew not how to show mercy. To escape his cruelty, I determined to go [to] Charles Town, and throw myself into the hands of the English. They received me readily, and I began to feel the happiness, liberty, of which I knew nothing before, altho' I was grieved at first, to be obliged to leave my friends, and reside among strangers.

In this situation I was seized with the smallpox, and suffered great hardships; for all the Blacks affected with that disease, were ordered to be carried a mile from the camp, lest the soldiers should be infected, and disabled from marching. This was a grievous circumstance to me and many others. We lay sometimes a whole day without any thing to eat or drink; but Providence sent a man, who belonged to the York volunteers whom I was acquainted with, to my relief. He brought me such things as I stood in need of; and by the blessing of the Lord I began to recover. . . .

When I arrived at New-York, my friends rejoiced to see me once more restored to liberty, and joined me in praising the Lord for his mercy and goodness. But notwithstanding this great deliverance, and the promises I had made to serve God, yet my good resolutions soon vanished away like the morning dew: The love of this world extinguished my good desires, and stole away my heart from God, so that I rested in a mere form of religion for near three years. About which time, (in 1783) the horrors and devastation of war happily terminated, and peace was restored between America and Great Britain, which diffused universal joy among all parties, except us, who had escaped from slavery and taken refuge in the English army; for a report prevailed at New-York, that all the slaves, in number 2000, were to be delivered up to their masters, altho' some of them had been three or four years among the English. This dreadful rumour filled us all

Source: Boston King, "Memoirs of the Life of Boston King, A Black Preacher," *The Methodist Magazine* 21 (March 1798): 106–10, and 21 (April 1798): 15.

with inexpressible anguish and terror, especially when we saw our old masters coming from Virginia, North Carolina, and other parts, and seizing upon their slaves in the streets of New-York, or even dragging them out of their beds. Many of the slaves had very cruel masters, so that the thoughts of returning home with them embittered life to us. For some days we lost our appetite for food, and sleep departed from our eyes.

The English had compassion upon us in the day of distress, and issued out a Proclamation, importing, That all slaves should be free, who had taken refuge in the British lines, and claimed the sanction and privileges of the Proclamations respecting the security and protection of Negroes. In consequence of this, each of us received a certificate from the commanding officer at New-York, which dispelled all our fears, and filled us with joy and gratitude. Soon after, ships were fitted out, and furnished with every necessary for conveying us to Nova Scotia. We arrived at Burch Town in the month of August, where we all safely landed. Every family had a lot of land, and we exerted all our strength in order to build comfortable huts before the cold weather set in.

INTERPRET THE EVIDENCE

1. Why does Joseph Galloway oppose independence (Document 6.1)? How does he defend Great Britain? Does he believe the colonies owe something to the crown? What does he think will occur if the Continental Congress abandons a moderate course?

2. Why, according to Charles Inglis, should the colonists reunite with Great Britain (Document 6.2)? Why does he argue that the colonists need the crown? What does he predict will happen if reconciliation does not occur?

3. How does Hannah Griffits describe Thomas Paine (Document 6.3)? What does she claim is Paine's motivation for his writing? How does her critique compare to that of Inglis?

4. Why did Joseph Brant (Document 6.4) decide to remain loyal to the crown? How had the American colonists responded to the Mohawks' siding with the crown? What did Brant ask of the king?

5. What incident prompted Boston King to make an escape from slavery (Document 6.5)? What conditions did he find in the British camps? What were his experiences once the war ended? Is it accurate to refer to him as a loyalist?

PUT IT IN CONTEXT

1. What did these loyalists have in common? How did they differ? What factors do you think would have made a person more likely to side with Great Britain?

2. Do you think calls for reconciliation were realistic in 1775? In 1776? Why or why not?

The Whiskey Rebellion

In 1791 Alexander Hamilton, the first secretary of the treasury, sought a way to reduce the national debt, and he convinced Congress to pass the first internal revenue tax in the form of an excise tax on distilled spirits. This direct tax angered many Americans, especially farmers who turned their excess grain into whiskey, a lucrative and easily transported product. Their resentment increased because of provisions that taxed smaller producers at almost twice the rate as large producers and required that all stills be federally registered.

Farmers in western Pennsylvania were particularly resistant to the new tax. Many refused to pay the tax, and towns sent petitions to state and federal officials asking that the tax be repealed (Document 7.1). When this did not work, angry farmers resorted to violence. By the summer of 1794, the Whiskey Rebellion, as it became known, reached crisis state. Tax collectors were tarred and feathered, groups of farmers burned the homes of tax officials in western counties, and armed rebels attacked neighbors who supported the whiskey tax. Sympathetic residents in towns like Pittsburgh offered their support as farmers prepared for an armed confrontation (Document 7.2).

Washington and his cabinet feared that the revolt would become another Shays's Rebellion, and Hamilton described the rebels accordingly (Document 7.4). When the "whiskey rebels" refused to negotiate with government representatives, Washington placed the militias of four states under federal control (Document 7.3). When this force of 13,000 men arrived in Pennsylvania, however, most of the rebels had dispersed. The leaders were arrested and tried for treason, but only two leaders were convicted. Washington eventually pardoned all those involved in the revolt.

The Whiskey Rebellion was Washington's most serious domestic crisis and a test of the federal government's powers under the Constitution. Washington successfully defeated the rebels, but many Americans were outraged that force had been used against their fellow citizens. In response, Thomas Jefferson and James Madison, dissatisfied with this and other Federalist policies, formed the Democratic-Republican political party (Document 7.5).

DOCUMENT 7.1 | *Resolution to the Pennsylvania Legislature* (1791)

Throughout the summer of 1791, farmers in Pennsylvania met to discuss and protest the excise tax on whiskey. In September, representatives from several western counties met in Pittsburgh. There they drafted a resolution to be printed in the *Pittsburgh Gazette* and sent to the U.S. Congress and the Pennsylvania legislature. The following selection highlights the farmers' objections to the whiskey tax.

Resolved, That the said law is deservedly obnoxious to the feelings and interests of the people in general, as being attended with infringements on liberty, partial in its operations, attended with great expense in the collection, and liable to much abuse. It operates on a domestic manufacture, a manufacture not equal through the States. It is insulting to the feelings of the people to have their vessels marked, houses painted and ransacked, to be subject to informers, gaining by the occasional delinquency of others. It is a bad precedent tending to introduce the excise laws of Great Britain and of countries where the liberty, property, and even the morals of the people are sported with, to gratify particular men in their ambitious and interested measures.

Resolved, That in the opinion of this committee, the duties imposed by the said act on spirits distilled from the produce of the soil of the United States, will eventually discourage agriculture, and a manufacture highly beneficial in the present state of the country, that those duties which fall heavy, especially upon the western parts of the United States, which are, for the most part, newly settled, and where the aggregate of the citizens is of the laborious and poorer class, who have not the means of procuring the wines, spirituous liquors, etc., imported from foreign countries.

Source: Pennsylvania Archives, 2nd ser., 4:21.

DOCUMENT 7.2 | *The Pittsburgh Resolution* (1794)

As the Whiskey Rebellion reached a climax in the summer of 1794, its leaders called on armed volunteers to meet at Braddock's Field near Pittsburgh. At the same time, towns across western Pennsylvania held meetings to consider how best to support the rebels. Pittsburgh residents met on July 31 and drafted their own resolution to support the protesters, a portion of which follows.

In consequence of certain letters sent by the last mail, certain persons were discovered as advocates of the excise law, and enemies to the interests of the country,

Source: Pennsylvania Archives, 2nd ser., 4:21, 80–81.

and that a certain Edward Day, James Brison, and Abraham Kirkpatrick, were particularly obnoxious, and that it was expected by the country that they should be dismissed without delay; whereupon, it was resolved it should be so done, and a committee of twenty-one were appointed to see this resolution carried into effect.

Also, that, whereas it is a part of the message from the gentlemen of Washington, that a great body of the people of the country will meet to-morrow at Braddock's Field, in order to carry into effect measures that may seem to them advisable with respect to the excise law, and the advocates of it.

Resolved, That the above committee shall, at an early hour, wait upon the people on the ground, and assure the people that the above resolution, with respect to the proscribed persons, has been carried into effect.

Resolved, also, That the inhabitants of the town shall march out and join the people on Braddock's Field, as brethren, to carry into effect with them any measure that may seem to them advisable for the common cause.

Resolved, also, That we shall be watchful among ourselves of all characters that, by word or act, may be unfriendly to the common cause; and, when discovered, will not suffer them to live amongst us, but they shall instantly depart the town.

Resolved, That the town committee shall exist as a committee of information and correspondence, as an organ of our sentiments until our next town meeting. And that *whereas,* a general meeting of delegates from the townships of the country, on the west of the mountains, will be held at Parkinson's Ferry, on the Monongahela, on the 14th of August next.

Resolved, That delegates shall be appointed to that meeting, and that the 9th August next be appointed for a town meeting to elect such delegates.

DOCUMENT 7.3 | GEORGE WASHINGTON, *Proclamation against the Rebels* (1794)

In August 1794, President Washington met with his cabinet and the governor of Pennsylvania to formulate a response to the rebels' growing threat. Washington then issued a proclamation that called on the rebels and anyone "aiding, abetting, or comforting" them to end their revolt and return home. In the proclamation, Washington also utilized the Militia Act of 1792 to call up troops from Maryland, New Jersey, Pennsylvania, and Virginia to put down the rebellion.

And whereas, By a law of the United States, intitled "An Act to provide for calling forth the Militia to execute the laws of the Union; suppress insurrections and repel invasions," it is enacted that whenever the laws of the United States shall be opposed, or the execution thereof obstructed in any State by combinations too powerful to be suppressed by the ordinary course of judicial proceedings, or by

Source: Pennsylvania Archives, 2nd ser., 4:21, 125–27.

the powers vested in the Marshal by that act, the same being notified by an associate Justice or a district Judge, it shall be lawful for the President of the United States to call forth the Militia of such State to suppress such combinations, and to cause the laws to be duly executed. And if the Militia of a State where such combinations may happen, shall refuse or be insufficient to suppress the same, it shall be lawful for the President, if the Legislature shall not be in session, to call forth and employ such numbers of the Militia of any other State or States most convenient thereto, as may be necessary; and the use of the militia so to be called forth may be continued, if necessary, until the expiration of thirty days after the commencement of the ensuing session: *Provided, always*, That whenever it may be necessary, in the judgment of the President, to use the Militia force hereby directed to be called forth, the President shall forthwith, and previous thereto, by Proclamation, command such insurgents to disperse and retire peaceably to their respective abodes within the limited time: . . .

And whereas, it is, in my judgment, necessary under the circumstances of the case to take measures for calling forth the militia in order to suppress the combinations aforesaid, and to cause the laws to be duly executed, and I have accordingly determined so to do, feeling the deepest regret for the occasion, but withal the most solemn conviction that the essential interest of the Union demand it, that the very existence of the government and the fundamental principles of social order are materially involved in the issue, and that the patriotism and firmness of all good citizens are seriously called upon as occasion may require, to aid in the suppression of so fatal a spirit;

Wherefore, and in pursuance of the proviso above recited, I, George Washington, President of the United States, do hereby command all persons, being insurgents, as aforesaid, and all others whom it may concern, on or before the first day of September next to disperse and retire peaceably to their respective abodes. And I do moreover warn all persons whomsoever against aiding, abetting, or comforting the perpetrators of the aforesaid treasonable acts; and do require all officers and other citizens, according to their respective duties and the laws of the land, to exert their utmost endeavors to prevent and suppress such dangerous proceedings.

DOCUMENT 7.4 | ALEXANDER HAMILTON, *Letter to George Washington* (August 5, 1794)

Washington's military preparations resulted in large part from the increasing violence occurring in western Pennsylvania. Tax collectors in particular faced the wrath of angry farmers and other citizens sympathetic to their plight. In the following letter, Alexander Hamilton relays to Washington reports of the violence that had occurred since the rebellion began. He also offers his own explanation of the types of people responsible for attacking not only government officials but also anyone who offered any support for the whiskey tax.

Source: Pennsylvania Archives, 2nd ser., 4:21, 88–89.

Sometime in October 1791, an unhappy man of the name of Wilson, a stranger in the county and manifestly disordered in his intellects, imagining himself to be a collector of the revenue, or invested with some trust in relation to it, was so unlucky as to make inquiries concerning distillers who had entered their stills, giving out that he was to travel through the United States to ascertain and report to Congress the number of stills, etc. This man was pursued by a party in disguise, taken out of his bed, carried about five miles back to a smith's shop, stripped of his clothes, which were afterwards burnt, and having been himself inhumanly burnt in several places with a heated iron, was tarred and feathered and about day-light dismissed naked, wounded and otherwise in a very suffering condition. These particulars are communicated in a letter from the inspector of the revenue of the 17th of November, who declares that he had then himself seen the unfortunate maniac, the abuse of whom, as he expresses it, exceeded description and was sufficient to make human nature shudder. The affair is the more extraordinary as persons of weight and consideration in that county are understood to have been actors in it, and as the symptoms of insanity were, during the whole time of inflicting the punishment, apparent; the unhappy sufferer displaying the heroic fortitude of a man who conceived himself to be a martyr to the discharge of some important duty.

Not long after a person of the name of Roseberry underwent the humiliating punishment of tarring and feathering with some aggravations for having in conversation hazarded the very natural and just but unpalatable remark that the inhabitants of that county could not reasonably expect protection from a government whose laws they so strenuously opposed.

The audacity of the perpetrators of these excesses was so great that an armed banditti ventured to seize and carry off two persons who were witnesses against the rioters in the case of Wilson in order to prevent their giving testimony of the riot to a court then sitting or about to sit.

Designs of personal violence against the inspector of the revenue himself, to force him to a resignation, were repeatedly attempted to be put in execution by armed parties, but, by different circumstances, were frustrated.

DOCUMENT 7.5 | JAMES MADISON, *Letter to James Monroe* (December 4, 1794)

James Madison and Thomas Jefferson were the leading critics of the Federalist policies of George Washington and Alexander Hamilton. Washington's decision to raise an army to put down the western Pennsylvania rebels confirmed Madison's fears that the national government had become too strong. In his letter to James Monroe, then serving as U.S. minister to France, Madison expresses his concern about Washington's use of military force and the dangers of a standing army. He also criticizes Federalist efforts to link rebellious farmers with the Republican societies (also sometimes called Democratic societies) established in support of the French Revolution and the emerging political opposition in the United States.

You will learn from the newspapers and official communications the unfortunate scene in the Western parts of Pennsylvania which unfolded itself during the recess. The history of its remote and immediate causes, the measures produced by it, and the manner in which it has been closed, does not fall within the compass of a letter. It is probable, also, that many explanatory circumstances are yet but imperfectly known. I can only refer to the printed accounts, which you will receive from the Department of State, and the comments which your memory will assist you in making on them. The event was, in several respects, a critical one for the cause of liberty, and the real authors of it, if not in the service, were, in the most effectual manner, doing the business of Despotism. You well know the general tendency of insurrections to increase the momentum of power. You will recollect the particular effect of what happened some years ago in Massachusetts. Precisely the same calamity was to be dreaded on a larger scale in this case. There were enough, as you may well suppose, ready to give the same turn to the crisis, and to propagate the same impressions from it. It happened most auspiciously, however, that, with a spirit truly Republican, the people every where, and of every description, condemned the resistance to the will of the majority, and obeyed with alacrity the call to vindicate the authority of the laws. You will see, in the answer of the House of Representatives to the President's speech, that the most was made of this circumstance, as an antidote to the poisonous influence to which Republicanism was exposed. If the insurrection had not been crushed in the manner it was, I have no doubt that a formidable attempt would have been made to establish the principle that a standing army was necessary for *enforcing the laws*. When I first came to this City, about the middle of October, this was the fashionable language. Nor am I sure that the attempt would not have been made, if the President could have been embarked in it, and particularly if the temper of New England had not been dreaded on this point. I hope we are over that danger for the present. You will readily understand the business detailed in the newspapers relating to the denunciation of the "self-created Societies." The introduction of it by the President was, perhaps, the greatest error of his political life. For his sake, as well as for a variety of obvious reasons, I wished it might be passed over in silence by the House of Representatives. The answer was penned with that view, and so reported. This moderate course would not satisfy those who hoped to draw a party advantage out of the President's popularity. The game was to connect the Democratic Societies with the odium of the insurrection; to connect the Republicans in Congress with those Societies; to put the President ostensibly at the head of the other party, in opposition to both, and by these means prolong the illusions in the North, and try a new experiment on the South. To favor the project, the answer of the Senate was accelerated, and so framed as to draw the President into the most pointed reply on the subject of the Societies. At the same time, the answer of the House of Representatives was procrastinated, till the example of the Senate and the commitment of the President could have their full operation. You will see how nicely the House was divided, and how the matter went off. As yet, the discussion has not been revived by the newspaper combatants. If it should, and equal talents be opposed, the result cannot fail to wound the President's popularity more than anything that has yet happened. It must be seen that no two principles can be either more indefensible in reason, or more dangerous in practice, than that—1. Arbitrary denunciations may punish what the law permits, and what the Legislature has no right by law to prohibit;

and that, 2. The Government may stifle all censure whatever on its misdoings; for if it be itself the Judge, it will never allow any censures to be just; and if it can suppress censures flowing from one lawful source, it may those flowing from any other—from the press and from individuals, as well as from Societies, &c.

The elections for the House of Representatives are over in New England and Pennsylvania. In Massachusetts, they have been contested so generally as to rouse the people compleatly from their lethargy, though not sufficiently to eradicate the errors which have prevailed there. The principal members have been all severely pushed; several changes have taken place, rather for the better, and *not one* for the worse.

INTERPRET THE EVIDENCE

1. What are the chief complaints of the whiskey rebels and their supporters (Documents 7.1 and 7.2)? Are they opposed only to the economic burden of a tax? Which of their arguments do you find the most convincing?

2. What argument does Washington make in favor of government action against the rebels (Document 7.3)? Do you find it convincing?

3. According to Hamilton's letter (Document 7.4), who was responsible for carrying out the violence of the Whiskey Rebellion? How does Hamilton characterize the attackers and the victims? How can we evaluate his claims?

4. On what basis does James Madison criticize President Washington's actions in response to the rebellion? Why does he believe that the Federalists' response to the rebellion is of greater concern than the rebellion itself (Document 7.5)?

5. Washington justified his use of force to put down the revolt by pointing to the violence employed by the rebels. What other strategies did the rebels use to protest the tax? How else might the federal government have responded to armed rebellion among its citizens?

PUT IT IN CONTEXT

1. What role did the Whiskey Rebellion play in the formation of a new political party?

2. What Democratic-Republican ideas are represented in the documents written by the whiskey rebels and their supporters, including James Madison?

DOCUMENT PROJECT 8

Race Relations in the Early Republic

In the late eighteenth century, the United States was far from extending the promises of equality and democracy championed in the Revolutionary War to all Americans. The majority of African Americans in the early Republic were enslaved, and eight of the first ten presidents were slaveholders. As cotton production expanded in the South, slavery did as well, and the slave population increased dramatically after 1790. With the end of the international slave trade in 1808, owners grew even more reluctant to free their slaves. As Andrew Jackson's 1804 ad for a runaway slave demonstrates (Document 8.2), slavery was a brutal system. The English Quaker Robert Sutcliff noted this physical brutality in his travels to Virginia and Pennsylvania (Document 8.3). While slave revolts were rare, those that occurred involved extensive planning, as suggested by the confession of a slave involved in one plot (Document 8.1).

Even free blacks lacked political and civil rights and suffered severe discrimination; however, some free blacks managed to create vibrant communities, as in Philadelphia. There African Americans agitated publicly against racism despite being denied the formal rights of citizenship (Document 8.4). In 1794, Richard Allen (Document 8.5) and other African Americans organized the St. Thomas African Methodist Episcopal Church of Philadelphia, the nation's first independent black church.

As you read the following documents, think about what they reveal about popular white perceptions of African Americans and what they suggest about how blacks sought to carve out a place for themselves in the early Republic.

DOCUMENT 8.1 | *Confession of Solomon* (September 1800)

Gabriel's Conspiracy was a plan for a massive slave rebellion in Virginia during the summer of 1800. The revolt's leader, Gabriel, was a slave and blacksmith on a tobacco plantation near Richmond who was often hired out to businesses in Richmond, where he recruited others to his plan. Gabriel was strongly influenced by the ideals of liberty advocated by participants in the American and Haitian Revolutions. When some of the slaves involved confessed the plan to their masters before the revolt began, Governor James Monroe ordered the state militia to round up the leaders

Source: H. W. Flournoy, ed., *Calendar of Virginia State Papers and Other Manuscripts from January 1, 1799, to December 31, 1807* (Richmond, 1890), 9:147.

of the conspiracy. Gabriel's brother Solomon was caught in the initial patrols and gave his confession, excerpted here, while several leaders were still at large. Gabriel was caught several weeks later, and Gabriel, Solomon, and twenty-five other slaves were executed for the conspiracy.

My brother Gabriel was the person who influenced me to join him and others in order that (as he said) we might conquer the white people and possess ourselves of their property. I enquired how we were to effect it. He said by falling upon them (the whites) in the dead of night, at which time they would be unguarded and unsuspicious. I then enquired who was at the head of the plan. He said Jack, alias Jack Bowler. I asked him if Jack Bowler knew anything about carrying on war. He replied he did not. I then enquired who he was going to employ. He said a man from Caroline who was at the siege of Yorktown, and who was to meet him (Gabriel) at the Brook and proceed on to Richmond, take, and then fortify it. This man from Caroline was to be commander and manager the first day, and then, after exercising the soldiers, the command was to be resigned to Gabriel. If Richmond was taken without the loss of many men they were to continue there some time, but if they sustained any considerable loss they were to bend their course for Hanover Town or York, they were not decided to which, and continue at that place as long as they found they were able to defend it, but in the event of a defeat or loss at those places they were to endeavor to form a junction with some negroes which, they had understood from Mr. Gregory's overseer, were in rebellion in some quarter of the country. This information which they had gotten from the overseer, made Gabriel anxious, upon which he applied to me to make scythe-swords, which I did to the number of twelve. Every Sunday he came to Richmond to provide ammunition and to find where the military stores were deposited. Gabriel informed me, in case of success, that they intended to subdue the whole of the country where slavery was permitted, but no further.

The first places Gabriel intended to attack in Richmond were, the Capitol, the Magazine, the Penitentiary, the Governor's house and his person. The inhabitants were to be massacred, save those who begged for quarter and agreed to serve as soldiers with them. The reason why the insurrection was to be made at this particular time was, the discharge of the number of soldiers, one or two months ago, which induced Gabriel to believe the plan would be more easily executed.

DOCUMENT 8.2 | ANDREW JACKSON, *Runaway Slave Advertisement* (1804)

Future president Andrew Jackson bought his first slaves in 1794 and by 1804 owned 9 slave men and women. In that same year, he bought the Hermitage, a Tennessee cotton plantation, and slowly increased the size of his property and its slave population. By the time he was president, he owned 100 slaves and would own more than 160 before his death in 1845. Although Jackson was known to provide adequate food and housing for his slaves, he was not above employing corporal punishment, as is evidenced by the following advertisement he placed for a runaway slave in 1804.

Source: *Tennessee Gazette*, November 7, 1804.

STOP THE RUNAWAY.
FIFTY DOLLARS REWARD.

Eloped from the subscriber, living near Nashville, on the 25th of June last, a Mulatto Man Slave, about thirty years old, six feet and an inch high, stout made and active, talks sensible, stoops in his walk, and has a remarkably large foot, broad across the root of the toes—will pass for a free man, as I am informed he has obtained by some means, certificates as such—took with him a drab great-coat, dark mixed body coat, a ruffled shirt, cotton home spun shirts, and overalls. He will make for Detroit, through the states of Kentucky and Ohio, or the upper part of Louisiana. The above reward will be given any person that will take him and deliver him to me or secure him in jail so that I can get him. If taken out of the state, the above reward, and all reasonable expenses paid—and ten dollars extra for every hundred lashes any person will give him to the amount of three hundred.

ANDREW JACKSON, near Nashville, State of Tennessee

DOCUMENT 8.3 | ROBERT SUTCLIFF, *Travels in Some Parts of North America* (1812)

Robert Sutcliff, an English Quaker, arrived in the United States on a business trip in 1804. Over the next three years, he recorded his travels in the country and published his experiences as a book in 1812. In the following excerpts, Sutcliff describes his encounters with the institution of slavery in the area around Richmond, Virginia, which include a reference to Gabriel's Conspiracy, and then in the last segment, near Philadelphia, Pennsylvania.

9th Month, 25th [1804].

I pursued my way to Richmond in the mail stage, through a beautiful country, but clouded and debased by Negro slavery. At the house where I breakfasted, which is called the Bowling-green, I was told that the owner had in his possession 200 slaves. In one field near the house, planted with tobacco, I counted nearly 20 women and children, employed in picking grubs from the plant. In the afternoon I passed by a field in which several poor slaves had lately been executed, on the charge of having an intention to rise against their masters. A lawyer who was present at their trials at Richmond, informed me that on one of them being asked what he had to say to the court on his defence, he replied in a manly tone of voice: "I have nothing more to offer than what General Washington would have had to offer, had he been taken by the British and put to trial by them. I have adventured my life in endeavouring to obtain the liberty of my countrymen, and am a willing sacrifice in their cause: and I beg, as a favour, that I may be immediately led to execution. I know that you have pre-determined to shed my blood, why then all this mockery of a trial?" . . .

Source: Robert Sutcliff, *Travels in Some Parts of North America, in the Years 1804, 1805, and 1806* (Philadelphia: B&T Kite, 1812), 50, 94, 181.

8th Month, 15th [1805].

I spent this day at Richmond. In the evening I walked to Manchester, over the bridge at James's River, which at this place is nearly half a mile wide. From my own observations, and the information I received from an inhabitant, Richmond appears to be a place of great dissipation; chiefly arising from the loose and debauched conduct of the white people with their black female slaves. It sometimes happens here, as in other places, that the white inhabitants, in selling the offspring of these poor debased females, sell their own sons and daughters with as much indifference as they would sell their cattle. By such means, every tender sentiment of the human breast is laid waste, and men become so degraded that their feelings rank but little above those of the beasts in the field. In their treatment of their offspring, how far do some of the brute creation surpass them! . . .

1st Month, 25th [1806].

In crossing the Schuylkill [River, at Philadelphia] on the floating bridge at the upper ferry, I passed a Negro boy apparently about 12 years of age. Round his neck an iron collar was locked, and from each side of it an iron bow passed over his head. His dress was a light linsey jacket and trowsers, without hat, shoes, or stockings. Soon after passing the boy, whom I supposed to be a runaway slave, I met a person of whom I inquired the reason of the boy's having so much iron about him. The man replied that the boy was his, and was so often running away that he had used that method to prevent him.

DOCUMENT 8.4 | *Free Blacks in Philadelphia Oppose Colonization* (1817)

Many African Americans fiercely resisted the idea of colonization—that free blacks and slaves should be returned to their ancestral homeland of Africa. The following document lists the resolutions of a group of prominent free blacks who met in Philadelphia in 1817 to express opposition to the American Colonization Society. The chair of the committee, sailmaker James Forten, was one of the wealthiest African Americans in the country.

Resolved unanimously, That the following address, signed on behalf of the meeting by the Chairman and Secretary, be published and circulated.

To the humane and benevolent Inhabitants of the city and county of Philadelphia.

The free people of color, assembled together, under circumstances of deep interest to their happiness and welfare, humbly and respectfully lay before you this expression of their feelings and apprehensions.

Source: William Lloyd Garrison, *Thoughts on African Colonization; or, An Impartial Exhibition of the Doctrines, Principles, and Purposes of the American Colonization Society, together with the Resolutions, Addresses, and Remonstrances of the Free People of Color* (Boston: Garrison and Knapp, 1832), part 2, 10–11.

Relieved from the miseries of slavery, many of us by your aid, possessing the benefits which industry and integrity in this prosperous country assure to all its inhabitants, enjoying the rich blessings of religion, by opportunities of worshipping the only true God, under the light of Christianity, each of us according to his understanding; and having afforded to us and to our children the means of education and improvement; we have no wish to separate from our present homes for any purpose whatever. Contented with our present situation and condition, we are not desirous of increasing their prosperity but by honest efforts, and by the use of those opportunities for their improvement, which the constitution and laws allow to all. It is therefore with painful solicitude and sorrowing regret we have seen a plan for colonizing the free people of color of the United States on the coast of Africa brought forward under the auspices and sanction of gentlemen whose names give value to all they recommend, and who certainly are among the wisest, the best, and the most benevolent of men in this great nation.

If the plan of colonizing is intended for our benefit and those who now promote it will never seek our injury; we humbly and respectfully urge that it is not asked for by us nor will it be required by any circumstances, in our present or future condition; as long as we shall be permitted to share the protection of the excellent laws and just government which we now enjoy, in common with every individual of the community.

We, therefore, a portion of those who are the objects of this plan, and among those whose happiness, with that of others of our color, it is intended to promote; with humble and grateful acknowledgements to those who have devised it, renounce and disclaim every connexion with it; and respectfully but firmly declare our determination not to participate in any part of it.

If this plan of colonization now proposed, is intended to provide a refuge and a dwelling for a portion of our brethren, who are now held in slavery in the south, we have other and stronger objections to it, and we entreat your consideration of them.

The ultimate and final abolition of slavery in the United States, by the operation of various causes, is, under the guidance and protection of a just God, progressing. Every year witnesses the release of numbers of the victims of oppression, and affords new and safe assurances that the freedom of all will be in the end accomplished. As they are thus by degrees relieved from bondage, our brothers have opportunities for instruction and improvement; and thus they become in some measure fitted for their liberty. Every year, many of us have restored to us by the gradual, but certain march of the cause of abolition — parents, from whom we have long been separated — wives and children whom we had left in servitude — and brothers, in blood as well as in early sufferings, from whom we had been long parted.

But if the emancipation of our kindred shall, when the plan of colonization shall go into effect, be attended with transportation to a distant land, and shall be granted on no other condition; the consolation for our past sufferings and of those of our color who are in slavery, which have hitherto been, and under the present situation of things would continue to be, afforded to us and to them, will cease for ever. The cords, which now connect them with us, will be stretched by the distance to which their ends will be carried, until they break; and all the sources of happiness, which affection and connexion and blood bestow, will be ours and theirs no more.

DOCUMENT 8.5 | RICHARD ALLEN, Excerpt from *The Life, Experience, and Gospel Labours of the Rt. Rev. Richard Allen* (1833)

Richard Allen was born a slave but purchased his own freedom in 1780, an opportunity he received after his master converted to Methodism and began to shift his opinion on slavery. Shortly after gaining his freedom, Allen became a traveling Methodist preacher. In the following document, he describes the circumstances that led to the founding of the first independent black church in the United States.

A number of us usually attended St. George's Church in Fourth street; and when the coloured people began to get numerous in attending the church, they moved us from the seats we usually sat on, and placed us around the wall, and on Sabbath morning we went to church and the sexton stood at the door, and told us to go in the gallery. He told us to go, and we would see where to sit. We expected to take the seats over the ones we formerly occupied below, not knowing any better. We took those seats. Meeting had begun, and they were nearly done singing, and just as we got to the seats, the elder said, "let us pray." We had not been long upon our knees before I heard considerable scuffling and low talking. I raised my head up and saw one of the trustees, H— M—, having hold of the Rev. Absalom Jones,[1] pulling him up off of his knees, and saying, "You must get up—you must not kneel here." Mr. Jones replied, "wait until prayer is over." Mr. H— M— said "no, you must get up now, or I will call for aid and I force you away." Mr. Jones said, "wait until prayer is over, and I will get up and trouble you no more." With that he beckoned to one of the other trustees, Mr. L— S— to come to his assistance. He came, and went to William White to pull him up. By this time prayer was over, and we all went out of the church in a body, and they were no more plagued with us in the church. This raised a great excitement and inquiry among the citizens, in so much that I believe they were ashamed of their conduct. But my dear Lord was with us, and we were filled with fresh vigour to get a house erected to worship God in. Seeing our forlorn and distressed situation, many of the hearts of our citizens were moved to urge us forward; notwithstanding we had subscribed largely towards finishing St. George's Church, in building the gallery and laying new floors, and just as the house was made comfortable, we were turned out from enjoying the comforts of worshiping therein. We then hired

---

Source: Richard Allen, *The Life, Experience, and Gospel Labours of the Rt. Rev. Richard Allen* (Philadelphia: Martin & Boden, 1833).

[1] **Rev. Absalom Jones**: Abolitionist and first African American Episcopalian priest.

a store room, and held worship by ourselves. Here we were pursued with threats of being disowned, and read publicly out of meeting if we did continue worship in the place we had hired; but we believed the Lord would be our friend. We got subscription papers out to raise money to build the house of the Lord. By this time we had waited on Dr. Rush[2] and Mr. Robert Ralston,[3] and told them of our distressing situation. We considered it a blessing that the Lord had put it into our hearts to wait upon those gentlemen. They pitied our situation, and subscribed largely towards the church, and were very friendly towards us, and advised us how to go on. We appointed Mr. Ralston our treasurer. Dr. Rush did much for us in public by his influence. I hope the name of Dr. Benjamin Rush and Mr. Robert Ralston will never be forgotten among us. They were the two first gentlemen who espoused the cause of the oppressed, and aided us in building the house of the Lord for the poor Africans to worship in. Here was the beginning and rise of the first African church in America.

But the elder of the Methodist church still pursued us. Mr. J— M— called upon us and told us if we did not erase our names from the subscription paper, and give up the paper, we would be publicly turned out of meeting. We asked him if we had violated any rules of discipline by so doing. He replied, "I have the charge given to me by the Conference, and unless you submit I will read you publicly out of meeting." We told him we were willing to abide by the discipline of the Methodist church; "and if you will show us where we have violated any law of discipline of the Methodist church, we will submit; and if there is no rule violated in the discipline, we will proceed on." He replied, "we will read you all out." We told him if he turned us out contrary to rule of discipline, we should seek further redress. We told him we were dragged off of our knees in St. George's church, and treated worse than heathens; and we were determined to seek out for ourselves, the Lord being our helper. He told us we were not Methodists, and left us. Finding we would go on in raising money to build the church, he called upon us again, and wished to see us all together. We met him. He told us that he wished us well, and that he was a friend to us, and used many arguments to convince us that we were wrong in building a church. We told him we had no place of worship; and we did not mean to go to St. George's church any more, as we were so scandalously treated in the presence of all the congregation present; "and if you deny us your name, you cannot seal up the scriptures from us, and deny us a name in heaven. We believe heaven is free for all who worship in spirit and truth." And he said, "so you are determined to go on." We told him—"yes, God being our helper." He then replied, "we will disown you all from the Methodist connexion." We believed if we put our trust in the Lord, he would stand by us. This was a trial that I never had to pass through before. I was confident that the great head of the church would support us. My dear Lord was with us. We went out with our subscription paper, and met with great success.

---

[2]**Dr. Rush**: Benjamin Rush, Philadelphia physician, chemistry professor, and reformer who signed the Declaration of Independence.

[3]**Mr. Robert Ralston**: Philadelphia merchant.

We had no reason to complain of the liberality of the citizens. The first day the Rev. Absalom Jones and myself went out we collected three hundred and sixty dollars. This was the greatest day's collection that we met with.

INTERPRET THE EVIDENCE

1. What encouraged slaves to revolt (Documents 8.1 and 8.3)? What do these documents reveal about slavery in Richmond and in Virginia more generally?

2. What does the runaway slave advertisement (Document 8.2) tell us about Andrew Jackson as a slave owner? Does the fact that it was written by a future president shape how you view it? Why or why not?

3. What does Robert Sutcliff's report (Document 8.3) reveal about the treatment that slaves in the North and in the South endured? Judging from his writing, how does Sutcliff's English and Quaker background affect his views of slavery?

4. Given the horrors of slavery in the North and the South and the near impossibility of overthrowing the institution, why did free blacks in Philadelphia oppose colonization (Document 8.4)? What language did they use to address their audience?

5. What caused Richard Allen (Document 8.5) and his colleagues to abandon St. George's Church? What did white Methodist ministers think of Allen's plan to organize a new church? What challenges did the founders of the new St. Thomas Church face?

PUT IT IN CONTEXT

1. According to these documents, how did race relations and the slave system in the United States change between 1785 and 1817?

DOCUMENT PROJECT 9

The Panic of 1819

The panic of 1819 lasted more than four years and was the first serious economic recession faced by the United States. It resulted primarily from irresponsible banking practices and the declining demand for cotton, food-stuffs, and other American goods in Europe. This combination prompted farm foreclosures, factory layoffs, bank failures, and widespread personal and business bankruptcies. In every region of the country, people were left jobless, homeless, and destitute, and thousands auctioned off their house-hold goods or were thrown into debtors' prisons (Documents 9.1 and 9.2). Private charities were overwhelmed, and most could not meet the demand for clothes, housing, and food.

In the midst of this tremendous suffering, the public focused its blame on bankers and government officials. There was much disagreement, how-ever, about the proper remedy for the economic recession. Some sought permanent restriction of bank credit, whereas others believed that cheaper credit would enable the economy to grow. Proposals were put forward to give direct government relief to debtors, abolish debtors' prisons, and start public works projects. Debates over whether to increase protective tariffs revealed the sectional differences emerging in the United States. In 1816 Congress had passed a tariff raising duties on foreign imports, and during the panic northern manufacturers wanted this tariff increased to further protect the U.S. market from foreign competition. Southern planters, on the other hand, blamed tariffs for raising the costs of manufactured goods and felt they benefited the North at the expense of the South (Document 9.3). The panic also led to calls for political reforms, especially by those who felt the government was not responsive to the needs of the laboring classes. Many states considered lowering or even abolishing property qualifica-tions for eligible voters. Documents 9.4 and 9.5 demonstrate both sides of this debate as it was taken up at the New York constitutional convention in 1821. By 1823 the panic had ended, but the economic and political changes it engendered reshaped American society and politics and would influence future responses to economic crises.

DOCUMENT 9.1 | *Auction in Chatham Square* (1820)

Cities throughout the United States were hit hard by the panic, and in the first year of the crisis the number of paupers in New York City increased from 8,000 to 13,000. Widespread unemployment resulted in evictions and homelessness for thousands of families. The following image of Chatham Square in lower Manhattan, painted in 1843, reveals a common scene in urban areas—the public auction of goods from an evicted family. Artist E. Didier depicted Chatham Square as it was in 1820, the last year auctions were held there as the area became increasingly residential.

© Museum of the City of New York, USA/Bridgeman Images

DOCUMENT 9.2 | JAMES FLINT, *Account of the Panic* (1820)

The Scottish traveler James Flint was touring America when the panic hit. In his letters home, he described the impact of the economic recession on banks, factories, and merchants. The following passage is from a letter he wrote from Jeffersonville, Indiana, describing the impossible conditions that many American workers faced.

Source: Reuben Gold Thwaites, ed., *Early Western Travels, 1748–1846* (Cleveland: Arthur H. Clark, 1904), 9:226–28, 236.

Merchants in Cincinnati, as elsewhere, have got into debt, by buying property, or by building houses, but are now secure in the possession. Such people, notwithstanding complain of the badness of the times, finding that the trade of buying without paying cannot be continued. Those who have not already secured an independence for life, may soon be willing to have trade and fair dealing as formerly. Property laws deprive creditors of the debts now due to them; but they cannot force them to give credit as they were wont to do.

Agriculture languishes—farmers cannot find profit in hiring labourers. The increase of produce in the United States is greater than any increase of consumpt that may be pointed out elsewhere. To increase the quantity of provisions, then, without enlarging the numbers of those who eat them, will be only diminishing the price farther. Land in these circumstances can be of no value to the capitalist who would employ his funds in farming. The spare capital of farmers is here chiefly laid out in the purchase of lands.

Labourers and mechanics are in want of employment. I think I have seen upwards of 1,500 men in quest of work within eleven months past, and many of these declared, that they had no money. Newspapers and private letters agree in stating, that wages are so low as eighteen and three-fourth cents (about tenpence) per day, with board, at Philadelphia, and some other places. Great numbers of strangers lately camped in the open field near Baltimore, depending on the contributions of the charitable for subsistence. You have no doubt heard of emigrants returning to Europe without finding the prospect of a livelihood in America. Some who have come out to this part of the country do not succeed well. Labourers' wages are at present a dollar and an eighth part per day. Board costs them two three-fourths or three dollars per week, and washing three-fourths of a dollar for a dozen of pieces. On these terms, it is plain that they cannot live two days by the labour of one, with the other deductions which are to be taken from their wages. Clothing, for example, will cost about three times its price in Britain: and the poor labourer is almost certain of being paid in depreciated money; perhaps from thirty to fifty per cent. under par. I have seen several men turned out of boarding houses, where their money would not be taken. They had no other resource left but to lodge in the woods, without any covering except their clothes. They set fire to a decayed log, spread some boards alongside of it for a bed, laid a block of timber across for a pillow, and pursued their labour by day as usual. . . .

Employers are also in the habit of deceiving their workmen, by telling them that it is not convenient to pay wages in money, and that they run accounts with the storekeeper, the tailor, and the shoemaker, and that from them they may have all the necessities they want very cheap. The workman who consents to this mode of payment procures orders from the employer, on one or more of these citizens, and is charged a higher price for the goods than the employer actually pays for them. This is called *paying in trade*. . . .

In the district of Jeffersonville, there has been an apparent interruption of the prosperity of the settlers. Upwards of two hundred quarter sections of land are by law forfeited to the government, for non-payment of part of the purchase money due more than a year ago. A year's indulgence was granted by Congress, but unless farther accommodation is immediately allowed, the lands will soon be offered a second time for sale. Settlers seeing the danger of losing their possessions are now offering to transfer their rights for less sums than have already been paid; it being still in the power of purchasers to retain the lands on paying up the arrears due in the land office. This marks the difficulty that individuals at present have in procuring small sums of money in this particular district.

DOCUMENT 9.3 | VIRGINIA AGRICULTURAL SOCIETY, *Antitariff Petition* (1820)

As political debates raged on whether to raise the protective tariff on imported goods, many groups around the country wrote Congress to support or protest the tariff. Most southern planters and farmers spoke out against the tariff, including the Virginia Agricultural Society of Fredericksburg. In January 1820, the organization sent a petition to Congress, from which the following selection is taken. In the aftermath of the panic, Congress passed the tariff of 1824, which raised duties on foreign imports.

That hostility, resulting from true republican principles, to partial taxation, exclusive privileges, and monopolies created by law, was the primary cause of our glorious and ever-memorable revolution.

That, although most of us are only the descendants of those patriots who achieved that revolution, by the lavish expenditure of their treasure and their blood, yet that we inherit enough of their spirit to feel equal aversion to similar oppressions; at the same time, we confidently trust that neither we, nor our sons after us, will ever be found backward or reluctant in offering up at the shrine of national good and national happiness any sacrifices, however great, which *their* promotion and preservation may obviously and necessarily require. But we have been taught to believe that a parental Government—a Government founded upon the immutable and sacred principles of truth, justice, and liberty—if she required sacrifices at all from those whom she is so solemnly bound to protect, would make them such as should operate equally upon every member of the community.

That we view with great concern, both nationally and individually, certain late attempts, on the part of various descriptions of domestic manufacturers, to induce your honorable body to increase the duties upon imports, already so high as to amount, upon many articles, nearly to a prohibition. This increased cost upon some of these may truly be designated a tax upon knowledge, if not a bounty to ignorance; such, for example, as the duty upon books in foreign languages, and upon philosophical, mathematical, surgical, and chemical instruments.

That, although these attempts are sustained under the plausible pretext of "promoting national industry," they are calculated (we will not say in *design*, but certainly in *effect*) to produce a tax highly impolitic in its nature, partial in

---

Source: "Remonstrance against Increase of Duties on Imports," House of Representatives, January 17, 1820, no. 570, 16th Cong., 1st sess., *American State Papers: Finance*, 3:447–48.

its operation, and oppressive in its effects: a tax, in fact, to be levied principally on the great body of agriculturists, who constitute a large majority of the whole American people, and who are the chief consumers of all foreign imports.

That such a tax would be a flagrant violation of the soundest and most important principles of political economy, amongst which we deem the following to be incontrovertibly true: that, as the interests of dealers and consumers necessarily conflict with each other, the first always aiming to *narrow*, whilst the latter, who form the majority of every nation, as constantly endeavor to *enlarge* competition; by which enlargement alone extravagant prices and exorbitant profits are prevented, it is the duty of every wise and just government to secure the consumers against both exorbitant profits and extravagant prices by leaving competition as free and open as possible.

DOCUMENT 9.4 | JAMES KENT, *Arguments against Expanding Male Voting Rights* (1821)

The economic crisis spawned debates throughout the country about the political system and its responsiveness to all classes of American citizens. The New York constitutional convention of 1821 included a committee that reviewed the state's voting laws and considered implementing "universal suffrage," that is, granting voting rights to all white men regardless of wealth or property. The committee heard testimony from supporters and opponents of property qualifications for voting. Chief Justice and Chancellor James Kent of New York argued in favor of property qualifications.

I have reflected upon the report of the select committee with attention and with anxiety. We appear to be disregarding the principles of the constitution, under which we have so long and so happily lived, and to be changing some of its essential institutions. . . .

The tendency of universal suffrage is to jeopardize the rights of property and the principles of liberty. . . .

The notion that every man that works a day on the road, or serves an idle hour in the militia, is entitled as of right to an equal participation in the whole power of the government is most unreasonable and has no foundation in justice. We had better at once discard from the report such a nominal test of merit. If such persons have an equal share in one branch of the legislature, it is surely as much as they can in justice or policy demand. Society is an association for the protection of property as well as of life, and the individual who contributes only one cent to the common stock ought not to have the same power and influence in directing the property concerns of the partnership as he who contributes his thousands. He will not have the same inducements to care, and diligence, and fidelity. His inducements and his temptation would be to divide the whole capital upon the principles of agrarian law [to ensure a more equal distribution of land to all classes].

Source: *Report of the Proceedings and Debates of the Convention of 1821* (Albany, 1821), 219, 221–22.

Liberty, rightly understood, is an inestimable blessing, but liberty without wisdom, and without justice, is no better than wild and savage licentiousness. The danger which we have hereafter to apprehend, is not the want, but the abuse, of liberty. We have to apprehend the oppression of minorities, and a disposition to encroach on private right—to disturb chartered privileges—and to weaken, degrade, and overawe the administration of justice; we have to apprehend the establishment of unequal, and consequently, unjust systems of taxation, and all the mischiefs of a crude and mutable legislation. A stable senate, exempted from the influence of universal suffrage, will powerfully check these dangerous propensities.

DOCUMENT 9.5 | NATHAN SANFORD, *Arguments for Expanding Male Voting Rights* (1821)

Nathan Sanford, a former U.S. senator and a delegate to the New York constitutional convention, argued in favor of removing property qualifications. Sanford and his supporters won the debate, and property qualifications were removed for white male voters. However, property qualifications were increased for black male voters, thus denying most African Americans the right to vote in the state.

The question before us is the right of suffrage—who shall, or who shall not, have the right to vote. The committee have presented the scheme they thought best; to abolish all existing distinctions and make the right of voting uniform. Is this not right? Where did these distinctions arise? They arose from British precedents. In England, they have their three estates, which must always have their separate interests represented. Here there is but one estate—the people. To me, the only qualifications seem to be the virtue and morality of the people; and if they may be safely entrusted to vote for one class of our rulers, why not for all? In my opinion, these distinctions are fallacious. We have the experience of almost all the other states against them. The principle of the scheme now proposed is that those who bear the burthens of the state should choose those that rule it. There is no privilege given to property, as such; but those who contribute to the public support, we consider as entitled to share in the election of rulers. . . .

. . . But how is the extension of the right of suffrage unfavourable to property? Will not our laws continue the same? Will not the administration of justice continue the same? And if so, how is private property to suffer? Unless these are changed, and upon them rest the rights and security of property, I am unable to perceive how property is to suffer by the extension of the right of suffrage. But we have abundant experience on this point in other states. Now, sir, in many states the right of suffrage has no restriction; every male inhabitant votes. Yet what harm has been done in those states? What evil has resulted to them from this cause? The course of things in this country is for

Source: *Report of the Proceedings and Debates of the Convention of 1821* (Albany, 1821), 178–79.

the extension and not the restriction of popular rights. I do not know that in Ohio or Pennsylvania, where the right of suffrage is universal, there is not the same security for private rights and private happiness as elsewhere.

INTERPRET THE EVIDENCE

1. How might images such as the one of the public auction (Document 9.1) have shaped public opinion about the panic?

2. How does James Flint (Document 9.2) describe the panic, and what comparisons does he make between American society and conditions in Europe?

3. On what grounds does the Virginia Agricultural Society of Fredericksburg protest the tariff (Document 9.3)? How does it place its struggles within the context of American history?

4. Compare the arguments of James Kent (Document 9.4) and Nathan Sanford (Document 9.5) in the debate over voting rights in New York. How do they conceptualize the principles of justice, rights, and equality? Which arguments do you find the most convincing, and why?

5. Do you think the members of the Virginia Agricultural Society would agree more with Nathan Sanford or with James Kent? Would they agree with James Flint or the creator of the public auction image?

PUT IT IN CONTEXT

1. How did the devastating impact of the panic of 1819 shape state- and national-level debates over economic policies and political rights?

2. How did the policies implemented during and immediately after the panic of 1819—particularly voting rights and tariff laws—change the U.S. political and economic landscape over the following decade?

DOCUMENT PROJECT 10

The Cherokee Removal

In 1830 Congress passed the Indian Removal Act, which allowed for the relocation of eastern Indians, such as the Cherokee, who lived in Georgia, to lands west of the Mississippi River. Over the previous decades, the Cherokee Indians had adopted "Americanization," as tribal leaders promoted Christianity, republican government, and domesticity in order to exist peacefully within the borders of the more powerful United States. Although these ideals seemingly aligned with those of Andrew Jackson, the president nevertheless championed removal (Document 10.1), arguing that the United States could not progress as long as the Indians lived in the East. The Cherokee Indians were also under assault from the government of the state of Georgia, which had initiated new plans to subjugate them. The tribe turned to the federal courts for relief, and the Supreme Court (Document 10.3) ruled on two significant Cherokee cases. In the end, however, the Court offered only a limited confirmation of Cherokee rights and did little to block federal removal plans.

The plight of the Cherokee Indians and other tribes subject to removal became a national topic of debate. The lithograph of Andrew Jackson as the Great Father (Document 10.4) offers one example of how discussions played out in the increasingly popular form of political cartoons. White men and women, primarily in the North, viewed Indian removal as an injustice and launched petition drives to fight the policy. Cherokee women participated in petitioning as well (Document 10.2).

Cherokee resistance could not stave off relocation. In December 1835, the Cherokee Treaty Party, a small, rogue group of Cherokees, signed the Treaty of New Echota, which exchanged Cherokee land for $68 million and 32 million acres of land in Indian Territory in the West. Cherokee chief John Ross (Document 10.5) was furious but could not convince Congress to reject the treaty. As a result, in 1838–1839 the U.S. government forced 15,000 Cherokees to abandon their homes and march to Indian Country in starvation conditions, a brutal Trail of Tears.

The following documents consider the question of Cherokee removal from different viewpoints: the federal government, the press, and the Cherokee Indians themselves. As you read, consider how these different voices envisioned the place of the Cherokee Nation in the American body politic.

DOCUMENT 10.1 | ANDREW JACKSON, *Second Annual Message* (1830)

In his second annual message before Congress, President Andrew Jackson outlined his case for Indian removal, explaining why he believed the process would benefit both white settlers and the Cherokee Indians.

The consequences of a speedy removal will be important to the United States, to individual States, and to the Indians themselves. The pecuniary advantages which it promises to the Government are the least of its recommendations. It puts an end to all possible danger of collision between the authorities of the General and State Governments on account of the Indians. It will place a dense and civilized population in large tracts of country now occupied by a few savage hunters. By opening the whole territory between Tennessee on the north and Louisiana on the south to the settlement of the whites it will incalculably strengthen the southwestern frontier and render the adjacent States strong enough to repel future invasions without remote aid. It will relieve the whole State of Mississippi and the western part of Alabama of Indian occupancy, and enable those States to advance rapidly in population, wealth, and power. It will separate the Indians from immediate contact with settlements of whites; free them from the power of the States; enable them to pursue happiness in their own way and under their own rude institutions; will retard the progress of decay, which is lessening their numbers, and perhaps cause them gradually, under the protection of the Government and through the influence of good counsels, to cast off their savage habits and become an interesting, civilized, and Christian community.

What good man would prefer a country covered with forests and ranged by a few thousand savages to our extensive Republic, studded with cities, towns, and prosperous farms embellished with all the improvements which art can devise or industry execute, occupied by more than 12,000,000 happy people, and filled with all the blessings of liberty, civilization and religion?

The present policy of the Government is but a continuation of the same progressive change by a milder process. The tribes which occupied the countries now constituting the Eastern States were annihilated or have melted

Source: President Jackson's Message to Congress "On Indian Removal," December 6, 1830; Records of the United States Senate, 1789–1990; Record Group 46; National Archives. http://www .ourdocuments.gov/doc.php?flash=true&doc=25&page=transcript.

away to make room for the whites. The waves of population and civilization are rolling to the westward, and we now propose to acquire the countries occupied by the red men of the South and West by a fair exchange, and, at the expense of the United States, to send them to land where their existence may be prolonged and perhaps made perpetual. Doubtless it will be painful to leave the graves of their fathers; but what do they more than our ancestors did or than our children are now doing? To better their condition in an unknown land our forefathers left all that was dear in earthly objects. Our children by thousands yearly leave the land of their birth to seek new homes in distant regions. Does Humanity weep at these painful separations from everything, animate and inanimate, with which the young heart has become entwined? Far from it. It is rather a source of joy that our country affords scope where our young population may range unconstrained in body or in mind, developing the power and facilities of man in their highest perfection. These remove hundreds and almost thousands of miles at their own expense, purchase the lands they occupy, and support themselves at their new homes from the moment of their arrival. Can it be cruel in this Government when, by events which it can not control, the Indian is made discontented in his ancient home to purchase his lands, to give him a new and extensive territory, to pay the expense of his removal, and support him a year in his new abode? How many thousands of our own people would gladly embrace the opportunity of removing to the West on such conditions! If the offers made to the Indians were extended to them, they would be hailed with gratitude and joy.

And is it supposed that the wandering savage has a stronger attachment to his home than the settled, civilized Christian? Is it more afflicting to him to leave the graves of his fathers than it is to our brothers and children? Rightly considered, the policy of the General Government toward the red man is not only liberal, but generous. He is unwilling to submit to the laws of the States and mingle with their population. To save him from this alternative, or perhaps utter annihilation, the General Government kindly offers him a new home, and proposes to pay the whole expense of his removal and settlement.

DOCUMENT 10.2 | *Petition of the Women's Councils to the Cherokee National Council* (1831)

As the Cherokee Indians adopted more "American" styles of culture and governance, women were less involved in leadership of the tribe. Still, they organized to make their voices heard. The following petition lends insight into how Cherokee women felt about the removal plans.

Source: *Cherokee Phoenix*, November 12, 1831, in *The Cherokee Removal: A Brief History with Documents*, ed. Theda Perdue and Michael Green, 2nd ed. (Boston: Bedford/St. Martin's, 2005), 134.

To the Committee and Council,

We the females, residing in Salequoree and Pine Log, believing that the present difficulties and embarrassments under which this nation is placed demands a full expression of the mind of every individual, on the subject of emigrating to Arkansas, would take upon ourselves to address you. Although it is not common for our sex to take part in public measures, we nevertheless feel justified in expressing our sentiments on any subject where our interest is as much at stake as any other part of the community.

We believe the present plan of the General Government to effect our removal West of the Mississippi, and thus obtain our lands for the use of the State of Georgia, to be highly oppressive, cruel, and unjust. And we sincerely hope there is no consideration which can induce our citizens to forsake the land of our fathers of which they have been in possession from time immemorial, and thus compel us, against our will, to undergo the toils and difficulties of removing with our helpless families hundreds of miles to unhealthy and unproductive country. We hope therefore the Committee and Council will take into deep consideration our deplorable situation, and do everything in their power to avert such a state of things. And we trust by a prudent course their transactions with the General Government will enlist in our behalf the sympathies of the good people of the United States.

DOCUMENT 10.3 | JOHN MARSHALL, *Majority Opinion,* Cherokee Nation v. Georgia (1831)

In two major cases, *Cherokee Nation v. Georgia* (1831) and *Worcester v. Georgia* (1832), the Court confirmed that the Cherokee Indians constituted a nation separate from the United States but, as Justice John Marshall's majority opinion in the 1831 case makes clear, placed limits on its independence and authority.

The Indian Territory is admitted to compose a part of the United States. In all our maps, geographical treatises, histories, and laws, it is so considered. In all our intercourse with foreign nations, in our commercial regulations, in any attempt at intercourse between Indians and foreign nations, they are considered as within the jurisdictional limits of the United States, subject to many of those restraints which are imposed upon our own citizens. They acknowledge themselves in their treaties to be under the protection of the United States; they admit that the United States shall have the sole and exclusive right of regulating the trade with them, and managing all their affairs as they think proper; and the Cherokees, in

Source: *Cherokee Nation v. Georgia*, 30 U.S. 1 (1831), https://www.law.cornell.edu/supremecourt/text/30/1.

particular, were allowed by the treaty of Hopewell, which preceded the Constitution, "to send a deputy of their choice, whenever they think fit, to Congress." Treaties were made with some tribes by the State of New York, under a then unsettled construction of the confederation by which they ceded all their lands to that State, taking back a limited grant to themselves in which they admit their dependence.

Though the Indians are acknowledged to have an unquestionable, and heretofore unquestioned right to the lands they occupy, until that right shall be extinguished by a voluntary cession to our government, yet it may well be doubted whether those tribes which reside within the acknowledged boundaries of the United States can, with strict accuracy, be denominated foreign nations. They may, more correctly, perhaps, be denominated domestic dependent nations. They occupy a territory to which we assert a title independent of their will, which must take effect in point of possession when their right of possession ceases. Meanwhile they are in a state of pupilage. Their relation to the United States resembles that of a ward to his guardian.

They look to our government for protection; rely upon its kindness and its power; appeal to it for relief to their wants; and address the President as their Great Father. They and their country are considered by foreign nations, as well as by ourselves, as being so completely under the sovereignty and dominion of the United States that any attempt to acquire their lands, or to form a political connexion with them, would be considered by all as an invasion of our territory and an act of hostility.

These considerations go far to support the opinion that the framers of our Constitution had not the Indian tribes in view when they opened the courts of the union to controversies between a State or the citizens thereof, and foreign states.

In considering this subject, the habits and usages of the Indians in their intercourse with their white neighbours ought not to be entirely disregarded. At the time the Constitution was framed, the idea of appealing to an American court of justice for an assertion of right or a redress of wrong had perhaps never entered the mind of an Indian or of his tribe. Their appeal was to the tomahawk, or to the Government. This was well understood by the Statesmen who framed the Constitution of the United States, and might furnish some reason for omitting to enumerate them among the parties who might sue in the courts of the union. Be this as it may, the peculiar relations between the United States and the Indians occupying our territory are such that we should feel much difficulty in considering them as designated by the term foreign state were there no other part of the Constitution which might shed light on the meaning of these words. But we think that, in construing them, considerable aid is furnished by that clause in the eighth section of the third article which empowers Congress to "regulate commerce with foreign nations, and among the several States, and with the Indian tribes."

In this clause, they are as clearly contradistinguished by a name appropriate to themselves from foreign nations as from the several States composing the union. They are designated by a distinct appellation, and as this appellation can be applied to neither of the others, neither can the appellation distinguishing either of the others be in fair construction applied to them. The objects to which the power of regulating commerce might be directed are divided into three distinct classes—foreign nations, the several States, and Indian tribes. When forming this article, the convention considered them as entirely distinct. We cannot assume that the distinction was lost in framing a subsequent article unless there be something in its language to authorize the assumption. . . .

The Court has bestowed its best attention on this question, and, after mature deliberation, the majority is of opinion that an Indian tribe or Nation within the United States is not a foreign state in the sense of the Constitution, and cannot maintain an action in the Courts of the United States.

A serious additional objection exists to the jurisdiction of the Court. Is the matter of the bill the proper subject for judicial inquiry and decision? It seeks to restrain a State from the forcible exercise of legislative power over a neighbouring people, asserting their independence, their right to which the State denies. On several of the matters alleged in the bill, for example, on the laws making it criminal to exercise the usual powers of self-government in their own country by the Cherokee Nation, this Court cannot interpose, at least in the form in which those matters are presented.

That part of the bill which respects the land occupied by the Indians, and prays the aid of the Court to protect their possession may be more doubtful. The mere question of right might perhaps be decided by this Court in a proper case with proper parties. But the Court is asked to do more than decide on the title. The bill requires us to control the Legislature of Georgia, and to restrain the exertion of its physical force. The propriety of such an interposition by the Court may be well questioned. It savours too much of the exercise of political power to be within the proper province of the judicial department. But the opinion on the point respecting parties makes it unnecessary to decide this question.

If it be true that the Cherokee Nation have rights, this is not the tribunal in which those rights are to be asserted. If it be true that wrongs have been inflicted, and that still greater are to be apprehended, this is not the tribunal which can redress the past or prevent the future.

The motion for an injunction is denied.

DOCUMENT 10.4 | *Andrew Jackson as the Great Father* (c. 1835)

Federal Indian policy was debated beyond the realm of government, as people expressed their support or opposition in a wide variety of venues, including the nation's newspapers. The following cartoon offers a satirical depiction of Andrew Jackson's relationship with the Cherokee Indians.

DOCUMENT 10.5 | JOHN ROSS, *On the Treaty of New Echota* (1836)

In the Treaty of New Echota, the Cherokee Indians relinquished their claims to their land east of the Mississippi River, apparently clearing the way for their removal westward. But did the Treaty Party, the group of Cherokees who negotiated the treaty with the U.S. government, possess the authority to make such a deal? Cherokee chief John Ross outlines his opposition to removal and illuminates the political fissures that had occurred among the Cherokee Indians.

It is well known that for a number of years past we have been harassed by a series of vexations, which it is deemed unnecessary to recite in detail, but the evidence of which our delegation will be prepared to furnish. With a view to bringing our troubles to a close, a delegation was appointed on the 23rd of October, 1835, by the General Council of the nation, clothed with full powers to enter into arrangements with the Government of the United States, for the final adjustment of all our existing difficulties. The delegation failing to effect an arrangement with the United States commissioner, then in the nation, proceeded, agreeably to their instructions in that case, to Washington City, for the purpose of negotiating a treaty with the authorities of the United States.

After the departure of the Delegation, a contract was made by the Rev. John F. Schermerhorn, and certain individual Cherokees, purporting to be a "treaty, concluded at New Echota, in the State of Georgia, on the 29th day of December, 1835, by General William Carroll and John F. Schermerhorn, commissioners on the part of the United States, and the chiefs, headmen, and people of the Cherokee tribes of Indians." A spurious Delegation, in violation of a special injunction of the general council of the nation, proceeded to Washington City with this pretended treaty, and by false and fraudulent representations supplanted in the favor of the Government the legal and accredited Delegation of the Cherokee people, and obtained for this instrument, after making important alterations in its provisions, the recognition of the United States Government. And now it is presented to us as a treaty, ratified by the Senate, and approved by the President [Andrew Jackson], and our acquiescence in its requirements demanded, under the sanction of the displeasure of the United States, and the threat of summary compulsion, in case of refusal. It comes to us, not through our legitimate authorities, the known and usual medium of communication between the Government of the United States and our nation, but through the agency of a complication of powers, civil and military.

By the stipulations of this instrument, we are despoiled of our private possessions, the indefeasible property of individuals. We are stripped of every attribute of freedom and eligibility for legal self-defence. Our property may be plundered before our eyes; violence may be committed on our persons; even our lives may be taken away, and there is none to regard our complaints. We are

---

Source: John Ross, *The Papers of Chief John Ross*, ed. Gary E. Moulton, vol. 1, *1807–1839* (Norman: University of Oklahoma Press, 1985), 458–61, http://www.pbs.org/wgbh/aia/part4/4h3083t .html.

denationalized; we are disfranchised. We are deprived of membership in the human family! We have neither land nor home, nor resting place that can be called our own. And this is effected by the provisions of a compact which assumes the venerated, the sacred appellation of treaty.

We are overwhelmed! Our hearts are sickened, our utterance is paralized, when we reflect on the condition in which we are placed, by the audacious practices of unprincipled men, who have managed their stratagems with so much dexterity as to impose on the Government of the United States, in the face of our earnest, solemn, and reiterated protestations.

The instrument in question is not the act of our Nation; we are not parties to its covenants; it has not received the sanction of our people. The makers of it sustain no office nor appointment in our Nation, under the designation of Chiefs, Head men, or any other title, by which they hold, or could acquire, authority to assume the reins of Government, and to make bargain and sale of our rights, our possessions, and our common country. And we are constrained solemnly to declare, that we cannot but contemplate the enforcement of the stipulations of this instrument on us, against our consent, as an act of injustice and oppression, which, we are well persuaded, can never knowingly be countenanced by the Government and people of the United States; nor can we believe it to be the design of these honorable and highminded individuals, who stand at the head of the Govt., to bind a whole Nation, by the acts of a few unauthorized individuals. And, therefore, we, the parties to be affected by the result, appeal with confidence to the justice, the magnanimity, the compassion, of your honorable bodies, against the enforcement, on us, of the provisions of a compact, in the formation of which we have had no agency.

In truth, our cause is your own; it is the cause of liberty and of justice; it is based upon your own principles, which we have learned from yourselves; for we have gloried to count your [George] Washington and your [Thomas] Jefferson our great teachers; we have read their communications to us with veneration; we have practised their precepts with success. And the result is manifest. The wildness of the forest has given place to comfortable dwellings and cultivated fields, stocked with the various domestic animals. Mental culture, industrious habits, and domestic enjoyments, have succeeded the rudeness of the savage state.

We have learned your religion also. We have read your Sacred books. Hundreds of our people have embraced their doctrines, practised the virtues they teach, cherished the hopes they awaken, and rejoiced in the consolations which they afford. To the spirit of your institutions, and your religion, which has been imbibed by our community, is mainly to be ascribed that patient endurance which has characterized the conduct of our people, under the laceration of their keenest woes. For assuredly, we are not ignorant of our condition; we are not insensible to our sufferings. We feel them! we groan under their pressure! And anticipation crowds our breasts with sorrows yet to come. We are, indeed, an afflicted people! Our spirits are subdued! Despair has well nigh seized upon our energies! But we speak to the representatives of a Christian country; the friends of justice; the patrons of the oppressed. And our hopes revive, and our prospects brighten, as we indulge the thought. On your sentence, our fate is suspended; prosperity or desolation depends on your word. To you, therefore, we look! Before your august assembly we present ourselves, in the attitude of deprecation, and of entreaty. On your kindness, on your humanity, on your compassion, on your benevolence, we rest our hopes. To you we address our reiterated prayers. Spare our people! Spare the wreck of our prosperity! Let not our deserted homes become the monuments of our desolation! But we forbear! We suppress the agonies which wring our hearts, when we look at our wives, our children, and our venerable sires! We restrain the forebodings of anguish and distress, of misery and devastation and death, which must be the attendants on the execution of this ruinous compact.

INTERPRET THE EVIDENCE

1. How does Andrew Jackson's argument for Indian removal (Document 10.1) reflect his vision of an ideal America? How does he characterize Indians, and what role does he see them playing in the nation's future?

2. Why, according to the Women's Councils (Document 10.2), was Indian removal unjust? How did these women consider their gender when making their argument?

3. According to Chief Justice John Marshall's opinion in *Cherokee Nation v. Georgia* (Document 10.3), what standing did the Cherokee Nation have in the eyes of the Supreme Court? What do Andrew Jackson's address and Marshall's opinion tell us about how the different branches of the federal government viewed the Cherokee Indians? What do these documents reveal about the relationship between the Cherokee Indians and the state governments?

4. Do you think the artist of the lithograph *Andrew Jackson as Great Father* (Document 10.4) would be more inclined to agree with Andrew Jackson's or John Ross's (Document 10.5) vision of Indian removal? What artistic techniques reveal his political intentions?

5. Why did John Ross (Document 10.5) dispute the validity of the Treaty of Echota? How did he appeal to American traditions in forming his critique? What do we learn about Ross's conception of the rights of citizenship from this document?

PUT IT IN CONTEXT

1. Did Indians have more in common with slaves or with free whites in terms of their rights and their relationship to the federal government?

2. How did race and ethnicity shape the ways in which Americans experienced westward expansion?

DOCUMENT PROJECT 11

Debating Abolition

When William Lloyd Garrison (Document 11.1) founded the *Liberator* in 1831 and organized the American Anti-Slavery Society (AASS) two years later, he helped initiate a new phase of the abolitionist movement. As the AASS gained supporters (as well as enemies) across the North and West, a critical split among abolitionists intensified. Garrison and many AASS members, including Stephen Symonds Foster (Document 11.3), argued for a more radical form of abolitionism. They demanded that slavery's spread be halted. In their view, whites in areas where slavery existed must agitate to end it, as Angelina Grimké (Document 11.2) argued in her widely read 1836 pamphlet *Appeal to the Christian Women of the South*. Perhaps most controversially, the Garrisonians argued that the Constitution itself upheld the system of slavery. In their view, the compact that undergirded the U.S. government was morally bankrupt and therefore "true" abolitionists should not participate in that government in any form.

Many other abolitionists—often referred to as political abolitionists—disagreed with this concept of the Constitution as an illegitimate proslavery document. While political abolitionists had often begun their antislavery careers in the AASS, by 1840 they had broken with that organization, believing that moral suasion was inadequate to defeat the South's "slavocracy." They insisted, instead, that the best way to bring slavery to an end was to enter the political realm, where the dominant Whig and Democratic Parties tried to ignore the slavery issue, particularly in national contests for the presidency. Political abolitionists formed the Liberty Party (Document 11.4) in 1840, and by mid-decade it constituted a significant force in American politics. Many Garrisonians, most notably Frederick Douglass (Document 11.5), eventually came around to the political argument. But political abolitionists still faced roadblocks, not only from radical abolitionists but also from within their own ranks. The Liberty Party itself split, with Gerrit Smith and others beginning a new organization, the Liberty League, to protest their former party's merger into the more moderate Free-Soil Party.

The following documents offer examples of both sides of the Garrisonian versus political abolitionism debate. As you read the documents, consider a question that arises in many great debates throughout American history: Can change best be effected through working within the system or through advocating its overthrow?

DOCUMENT 11.1 | WILLIAM LLOYD GARRISON, *On the Constitution and the Union* (1832)

William Lloyd Garrison's *Liberator* newspaper provided a voice for a new group of radical abolitionists. Garrison himself emerged as the nation's foremost radical critic of slavery. The role of the Constitution in protecting the slave system was one of his most frequent targets. The following editorial appeared in the *Liberator* on December 29, 1832.

There is much declamation about the sacredness of the compact which was formed between the free and slave states, on the adoption of the Constitution. A sacred compact, forsooth! We pronounce it the most bloody and heaven-daring arrangement ever made by men for the continuance and protection of a system of the most atrocious villainy ever exhibited on earth. Yes—we recognize the compact, but with feelings of shame and indignation; and it will be held in everlasting infamy by the friends of justice and humanity throughout the world. It was a compact formed at the sacrifice of the bodies and souls of millions of our race, for the sake of achieving a political object—an unblushing and monstrous coalition to do evil that good might come. Such a compact was, in the nature of things and according to the law of God, null and void from the beginning. No body of men ever had the right to guarantee the holding of human beings in bondage. Who or what were the framers of our government, that they should dare confirm and authorise such high-handed villainy—such a flagrant robbery of the inalienable rights of man—such a glaring violation of all the precepts and injunctions of the gospel—such a savage war upon a sixth part of our whole population?—They were men, like ourselves—as fallible, as sinful, as weak, as ourselves. By the infamous bargain which they made between themselves, they virtually dethroned the Most High God, and trampled beneath their feet their own solemn and heaven-attested Declaration, that all men are created equal, and endowed by their Creator with certain inalienable rights—among which are life, liberty, and the pursuit of happiness. They had no lawful power to bind themselves, or their posterity, for one hour—for one moment—by such an unholy alliance. It was not valid then—it is not valid now. Still they persisted in maintaining it—and still do their successors, the people of Massachusetts, of New-England, and of the twelve free States, persist in maintaining it. A sacred compact! a sacred compact! What, then, is wicked and ignominious?

Source: *Liberator*, December 29, 1832.

This, then, is the relation in which we of New-England stand to the holders of slaves at the south, and this is virtually our language toward them—"Go on, most worthy associates, from day to day, from month to month, from year to year, from generation to generation, plundering two millions of human beings of their liberty and the fruits of their toil—driving them into the fields like cattle—starving and lacerating their bodies—selling the husband from his wife, the wife from her husband, and children from their parents—spilling their blood—withholding the bible from their hands and all knowledge from their minds—and kidnapping annually sixty thousand infants, the offspring of pollution and shame! Go on, in these practices—we do not wish nor mean to interfere, for the rescue of your victims, even by expostulation or warning—we like your company too well to offend you by denouncing your conduct. . . . Go on, from bad to worse—add link to link to the chains upon the bodies of your victims—add constantly to the intolerable burdens under which they groan—and if, goaded to desperation by your cruelties; they should rise to assert their rights and redress their wrongs, fear nothing—we are pledged, by a sacred compact, to shoot them like dogs and rescue you from their vengeance! Go on—we never will forsake you, for 'there is honor among thieves'—our swords are ready to leap from their scabbards, and our muskets to pour forth deadly vollies, as soon as you are in danger. We pledge you our physical strength, by the sacredness of the national compact—a compact by which we have enabled you already to plunder, persecute and destroy two millions of slaves, who now lie beneath the sod; and by which we now give you the same piratical license to prey upon a much larger number of victims and all their posterity. Go on—and by this sacred instrument, the Constitution of the United States, *dripping as it is with human blood*, we solemnly pledge you our lives, our fortunes, and our sacred honor, that we will stand by you to the last."

DOCUMENT 11.2 | ANGELINA GRIMKÉ, *Appeal to the Christian Women of the South* (1836)

The Grimké sisters, Angelina and Sarah, opposed slavery and moved from their native Charleston to Philadelphia to take up the causes of abolitionism and women's rights. Angelina Grimké earned recognition among abolitionists for her letters to Garrison's *Liberator*, and in 1836 she issued a pamphlet that called for southern women to resist slavery from within. Whites in South Carolina burned the pamphlet.

But some slaveholders have said, "we were never in bondage to any man," and therefore the yoke of bondage would be insufferable to us, but slaves are accustomed to it, their backs are fitted to the burden. Well, I am willing to admit that you who have lived in freedom would find slavery even more oppressive than the poor slave does, but then you may try this question in another form—Am

Source: Angelina Grimké, "Appeal to the Christian Women of the South," *Anti-Slavery Examiner* 1, no. 2 (September 1836).

I willing to reduce my *little child* to slavery? You know that if *it is* brought up a slave it will never know any contrast, between freedom and bondage, its back will become fitted to the burden just as the negro child's does—*not by nature*—but by daily, violent pressure, in the same way that the head of the Indian child becomes flattened by the boards in which it is bound. It has been justly remarked that "God never made a slave," he made man upright; his back was not made to carry burdens, nor his neck to wear a yoke, and the man must be crushed within him, before his back can be fitted to the burden of perpetual slavery; and that his back is not fitted to it, is manifest by the insurrections that so often disturb the peace and security of slaveholding countries. Who ever heard of a rebellion of the beasts of the field; and why not? simply because they were all placed under the feet of man, into whose hand they were delivered; it was originally designed that they should serve him, therefore their necks have been formed for the yoke, and their backs for the burden; but not so with man, intellectual, immortal man! I appeal to you, my friends, as mothers; Are you willing to enslave your children? You start back with horror and indignation at such a question. But why, if slavery is no wrong to those upon whom it is imposed? why, if as has often been said, slaves are happier than their masters, freedom from the cares and perplexities of providing for themselves and their families? why not place *your children* in the way of being supported without your having the trouble to provide for them, or they for themselves? Do you not perceive that as soon as this golden rule of action is applied to *yourselves* that you involuntarily shrink from the test; as soon as *your* actions are weighed in *this* balance of the sanctuary that you *are found wanting*? Try yourselves by another of the Divine precepts, "Thou shalt love thy neighbor as thyself." Can we love a man *as* we love *ourselves if* we do, and continue to do unto him, what we would not wish any one to do to us? Look too, at Christ's example, what does he say *of* himself, "I came *not* to be ministered unto, but to minister." Can you for a moment imagine the meek, and lowly, and compassionate Saviour, *a slaveholder?* do you not shudder at this thought as much as at that of his being *a warrior?* But why, if slavery is not sinful?

DOCUMENT 11.3 | STEPHEN SYMONDS FOSTER, *The Brotherhood of Thieves* (1843)

New Hampshire reformer Stephen Symonds Foster studied for the ministry but left Union Theological Seminary when the faculty demanded he stop giving antislavery lectures. Throughout his career, he sought to hold the church accountable for what he viewed as its complicity in slavery. Foster's incendiary rhetoric thrilled his supporters and often led his opponents to respond with violence. In the following document, he describes a speech he gave in Nantucket in 1842 that provoked an antiabolitionist riot.

Source: Stephen Symonds Foster, *The Brotherhood of Thieves; or, A True Picture of the American Church and Clergy: A Letter to Nathaniel Barney of Nantucket* (Concord, NH: Parker Pillsbury, 1884), 8–12.

I said at your meeting, among other things, that the American church and clergy, as a body, were thieves, adulterers, man-stealers, pirates, and murderers; that the Methodist Episcopal church was more corrupt and profligate than any house of ill-fame in the city of New York; that the Southern ministers of that body were desirous of perpetuating slavery for the purpose of supplying themselves with concubines from among its hapless victims; and that many of our clergymen were guilty of enormities that would disgrace an Algerine pirate!! These sentiments called forth a burst of holy indignation from the *pious* and *dutiful* advocates of the church and clergy, which overwhelmed the meeting with repeated showers of stones and rotten eggs, and eventually compelled me to leave your island, to prevent the shedding of human blood. . . .

This violence and outrage on the part of the church were, no doubt, committed to the glory of God and the honor of religion, although the connection between rotten eggs and holiness of heart is not very obvious. . . . But are not the charges here alleged against the clergy strictly and literally true? I maintain that they are true to the very letter; that the clergy and their adherents are literally, and beyond all controversy, a "brotherhood of thieves;" and, in support of this opinion, I submit the following considerations:—

You will agree with me, I think, that slaveholding involves the commission of all the crimes specified in my first charge, viz., theft, adultery, man-stealing, piracy, and murder. But should you have any doubts on this subject, they will be easily removed by analyzing this atrocious outrage on the laws of God, and the rights and happiness of man, and examining separately the elements of which it is composed. Wesley, the celebrated founder of the Methodists, once denounced it as the "sum of all villainies." Whether it be the sum of *all* villainies, or not, I will not here express an opinion; but that it is the sum of at least *five*, and those by no means the least atrocious in the catalogue of human aberrations, will require but a small tax on your patience to prove.

1. Theft. To steal, is to take that which belongs to another, without his consent. Theft and robbery are, *morally*, the same act, differing only in form. Both are included under the command, "Thou shalt not steal;" that is, thou shalt not take thy neighbor's property. Whoever, therefore, either secretly or by force, possesses himself of the property of another, is a thief. Now, no proposition is plainer than that every man owns his own industry. He who tills the soil has a right to its products, and cannot be deprived of them but by an act of felony. This principle furnishes the only solid basis for the right of private or individual property; and he who denies it, either in theory or practice, denies that right, also. But every slaveholder takes the entire industry of his slaves, from infancy to gray hairs; they dig the soil, but he receives its products. No matter how kind or humane the master may be,—he lives by plunder. He is emphatically a freebooter; and, as such, he is as much more despicable a character than the common horse-thief, as his depredations are more extensive.

2. Adultery. This crime is disregard for the requisitions of marriage. The conjugal relation has its foundation deeply laid in man's nature, and its strict

observance is essential to his happiness. Hence Jesus Christ has thrown around it the sacred sanction of his written law, and expressly declared that the man who violates it, even by a lustful eye, is an adulterer. But does the slaveholder respect this sacred relation? Is he cautious never to tread upon forbidden ground? No! His very position makes him the minister of unbridled lust. By converting woman into a commodity to be bought and sold, and used by her claimant as his avarice or lust may dictate, he totally annihilates the marriage institution, and transforms the wife into what he very significantly terms a "BREEDER," and her children into "STOCK."

This change in woman's condition, from a free moral agent to a chattel, places her domestic relations entirely beyond her own control, and makes her a mere instrument for the gratification of another's desires. The master claims her body as his property, and, of course, employs it for such purposes as best suit his inclinations,—demanding free access to her bed; nor can she resist his demands but at the peril of her life. Thus is her chastity left entirely unprotected, and she is made the lawful prey of every pale-faced libertine who may choose to prostitute her! To place woman in this situation, or to retain her in it when placed there by another, is the highest insult that any one could possibly offer to the dignity and purity of her nature; and the wretch who is guilty of it deserves an epithet compared with which adultery is spotless innocence. *Rape* is his crime! death his desert,—if death be ever due to criminals! Am I too severe? Let the offence be done to a sister or daughter of yours; nay, let the Rev. Dr. Witherspoon, or some other *ordained* miscreant from the South, lay his vile hands on your own bosom companion, and do to her what he has done to the companion of another,—and what Prof. Stuart and Dr. Fisk say he may do, "without violating the Christian faith,"—and I fear not your reply. None but a moral monster ever consented to the enslavement of his own daughter, and none but fiends incarnate ever enslave the daughter of another. Indeed, I think the demons in hell would be ashamed to do to their fellow-demons what many of our clergy do to their own church members.

3. Man-stealing. What is it to steal a man? Is it not to claim him as your property? —to call him yours? God has given to every man an inalienable right to himself,—a right of which no conceivable circumstance of birth, or forms of law, can divest him; and he who interferes with the free and unrestricted exercise of that right, who, not content with the proprietorship of his own body, claims the body of his neighbor, is a man-stealer. This truth is self-evident. Every man, idiots and the insane only excepted, knows that he has no possible right to another's body; and he who persists, for a moment, in claiming it, incurs the guilt of man-stealing. The plea of the slave-claimant, that he has bought, or inherited, his slaves, is of no avail. What right had he, I ask, to purchase, or to inherit, his neighbors? The purchase, or inheritance of them as a legacy, was itself a crime of no less enormity than the original act of kidnapping. But every slaveholder, whatever his profession or standing in society may be, lays his felonious hands on the body and soul of his equal brother, robs him of himself, converts him into an article of merchandise, and leaves him a mere chattel personal in the hands of his claimants. Hence he is a kidnapper, or man-thief.

4. Piracy. The American people, by an act of solemn legislation, have declared the enslaving of human beings on the coast of Africa to be piracy, and have affixed to this crime the penalty of death. And can the same act be piracy in Africa, and not be piracy in America? Does crime change its character by changing longitude? Is killing, with malice aforethought, no murder, where there is no human enactment against it? Or can it be less piratical and Heaven-daring to enslave our own native countrymen, than to enslave the heathen sons of a foreign and barbarous realm? If there be any difference in the two crimes, the odds is in favor of the foreign enslaver. Slaveholding loses none of its enormity by a voyage across the Atlantic, nor by baptism into the Christian name. It is piracy in Africa; it is piracy in America; it is piracy the wide world over; and the American slaveholder, though he possess all the sanctity of the ancient Pharisees, and make prayers as numerous and long, is a *pirate* still; a base, profligate adulterer, and wicked contemner [condemner] of the holy institution of marriage; identical in moral character with the African slave-trader, and guilty of a crime which, if committed on a foreign coast, he must expiate on the gallows.

5. Murder. Murder is an act of the mind, and not of the hand. "Whosoever hateth his brother is a murderer." A man may kill,—that is his hand may inflict a mortal blow,—without committing murder. On the other hand, he may commit murder without actually taking life. The intention constitutes the crime. He who, with a pistol at my breast, demands my pocket-book or my life, is a murderer, whichever I may choose to part with. And is not he a murderer, who, with the same deadly weapon, demands the surrender of what to me is of infinitely more value than my pocket-book, nay, than life itself—my liberty—myself—my wife and children—all that I possess on earth, or can hope for in heaven? But this is the crime of which every slaveholder is guilty. He maintains his ascendency over his victims, extorting their unrequited labor, and sundering the dearest ties of kindred, only by the threat of extermination. With the slave, as every intelligent person knows, there is no alternative. It is submission or death, or, more frequently, protracted torture more horrible than death. Indeed, the South never sleeps, but on dirks, and pistols, and bowie knives, with a troop of blood-hounds standing sentry at every door!

DOCUMENT 11.4 | *Liberty Party Platform* (1844)

The Liberty Party tried to end slavery by running candidates and electing officials who supported its cause. The following document is an excerpt of its official platform for the 1844 elections. Liberty Party presidential candidate James G. Birney of New York received 2.3 percent of the popular vote, enough to help Democratic candidate James K. Polk defeat Whig candidate Henry Clay.

Source: J. M. H. Frederick, ed., *National Party Platforms of the United States Presidential Candidates Electoral and Popular Votes* (Akron, OH: J. M. H. Frederick, 1896), 14–16.

Liberty Platform.

1. *Resolved*, That human brotherhood is a cardinal principle of true democracy, as well as pure Christianity, which spurns all inconsistent limitations; and neither the political party which repudiates it, nor the political system which is not based upon it, can be truly democratic or permanent.

2. *Resolved*, That the Liberty party, placing itself upon this broad principle, will demand the absolute and unqualified divorce of the General Government from slavery, and also the restoration of equality of rights among men, in every State where the party exists, or may exist. . . .

4. *Resolved*, That the Liberty party has not been organized merely for the over-throw of slavery; its first decided effort must, indeed, be directed against slave-holding as the grossest and most revolting manifestation of despotism, but it will also carry out the principle of equal rights into all its practical consequences and applications, and support every just measure conducive to individual and social freedom.

5. *Resolved*, That the Liberty party is not a sectional party but a national party; was not originated in a desire to accomplish a single object, but in a comprehensive regard to the great interests of the whole country; is not a new party, nor a third party, but is the party of 1776, reviving the principles of that memorable era, and striving to carry them into practical application.

6. *Resolved*, That it was understood in the times of the Declaration and the Constitution, that the existence of slavery in some of the States was in deroga-tion of the principles of American liberty, and a deep stain upon the character of the country, and the implied faith of the States and the Nation was pledged that slavery should never be extended beyond its then existing limits, but should be gradually, and yet, at no distant day, wholly abolished by State authority. . . .

8. *Resolved*, That the faith of the States and the Nation thus pledged, has been shamefully violated by the omission, on the part of many of the States, to take any measures whatever for the abolition of slavery within their respective limits; by the continuance of slavery in the District of Columbia, and in the Territo-ries of Louisiana and Florida; by the legislation of Congress; by the protection afforded by national legislation and negotiation to slaveholding in American vessels, on the high seas, employed in the coastwise slave traffic; and by the extension of slavery far beyond its original limits, by acts of Congress admitting new slave States into the Union.

9. *Resolved*, That the fundamental truths of the Declaration of Independence, that all men are endowed by their Creator with certain inalienable rights, among which are life, liberty and the pursuit of happiness, was made the fundamental law of our National Government, by that amendment of the Constitution which declares that no person shall be deprived of life, liberty, or property, without due process of law. . . .

11. *Resolved*, That the General Government has under the Constitution no power to establish or continue slavery anywhere, and therefore that all treaties and acts of Congress establishing, continuing or favoring slavery in the District

of Columbia, in the Territory of Florida, or on the high seas, are unconstitutional, and all attempts to hold men as property within the limits of exclusive national jurisdiction ought to be prohibited by law.

12. *Resolved*, That the provision of the Constitution of the United States which confers extraordinary political powers on the owners of slaves, and thereby constituting the two hundred and fifty thousand slaveholders in the slave States a privileged aristocracy; and the provisions for the reclamation of fugitive slaves from service, are anti-republican in their character, dangerous to the liberties of the people and ought to be abrogated. . . .

15. *Resolved*, That the practice of the General Government, which prevails in the slave States, of employing slaves upon the public works instead of free laborers and paying aristocratic masters, with a view to secure or reward political services, is utterly indefensible and ought to be abandoned.

16. *Resolved*, That freedom of speech and of the press and the right of petition and the right of trial by jury are sacred and inviolable, and that all rules, regulations and laws in derogation of either are oppressive, unconstitutional and not to be endured by a free people.

17. *Resolved*, That we regard voting in an eminent degree as a moral and religious duty, which, when exercised, should be by voting for those who will do all in their power for immediate emancipation. . . .

19. *Resolved*, That we hereby give it to be distinctly understood by this Nation and the world that, as Abolitionists, considering that the strength of our cause lies in its righteousness, and our hope for it, in our conformity to the laws of God and our respect for the rights of man, we owe it to the Sovereign Ruler of the Universe, as a proof of our allegiance to Him, in all our civil relations and offices, whether as private citizens or public functionaries sworn to support the Constitution of the United States, to regard and to treat the third clause of the fourth article of that instrument, whenever applied to the case of a fugitive slave, as utterly null and void, and consequently as forming no part of the Constitution of the United States whenever we are called upon or sworn to support it.

DOCUMENT 11.5 | FREDERICK DOUGLASS, *Abolitionism and the Constitution* (1851)

As one of the nation's most recognized abolitionists, Frederick Douglass played a central role in the antislavery debate. Originally a Garrisonian, by 1851 Douglass had switched sides to support the political abolitionists' position. The American Anti-Slavery Society announced that no pro-Constitution newspaper should receive the support of the organization, prompting Douglass to announce publicly his shift in opinion. Garrison responded by declaring, "There is roguery somewhere." The following announcement appeared first in Douglass's *North Star* newspaper and was reprinted in the *Liberator* a week later.

Source: *North Star*, May 23, 1851, reprinted in *Liberator*, May 30, 1851.

Change of Opinion Announced

The debate on the resolution relative to anti-slavery newspapers [at the annual meeting of the American Anti-Slavery Society] assumed such a character as to make it our duty to define the position of the *North Star* in respect to the Constitution of the United States. The ground having been distinctly taken, that no paper ought to receive the recommendation of the American Anti-Slavery Society that did not assume the Constitution to be a pro-slavery document, we felt in honor bound to announce at once to our old anti-slavery companions that we no longer possessed the requisite qualification for their official approval and commendation; and to assure them that we had arrived at the firm conviction that the Constitution, construed in the light of well established rules of legal interpretation, might be made consistent in its details with the noble purposes avowed in its preamble; and that hereafter we should insist upon the application of such rules to that instrument, and demand that it be wielded in behalf of emancipation. The change in our opinion on this subject has not been hastily arrived at. A careful study of the writings of Lysander Spooner, of Gerrit Smith, and of William Goodell, has brought us to our present conclusion. We found, in our former position, that, when debating the question, we were compelled to go behind the letter of the Constitution, and to seek its meaning in the history and practice of the nation under it—a process always attended with disadvantages; and certainly we feel little inclination to shoulder disadvantages of any kind, in order to give slavery the slightest protection. In short, we hold it to be a system of lawless violence; that it *never was lawful, and never can be made so*; and that it is the first duty of every American citizen, whose conscience permits so to do, to use his *political* as well as his *moral* power for its overthrow. Of course, this avowal did not pass without animadversion, and it would have been strange if it had passed without some crimination [recrimination]; for it is hard for any combination or party to attribute good motives to any one who differs from them in what they deem a vital point. Brother Garrison at once exclaimed, "There is roguery somewhere!" but we can easily forgive this hastily expressed imputation, falling, as it did, from the lips of one to whom we shall never cease to be grateful, and for whom we have cherished (and do now cherish) a veneration only inferior in degree to that which we owe to our conscience and to our God.

INTERPRET THE EVIDENCE

1. Why did William Lloyd Garrison characterize the Constitution as a proslavery document (Document 11.1)? What, according to Garrison, were the goals of the Constitution's authors? How does he describe Northerners and Southerners?

2. What arguments does Angelina Grimké (Document 11.2) use to attempt to convince southern women that slavery is wrong? How does she characterize slaveholders? What makes this document an example of radical abolitionism?

3. What charges does Stephen Symonds Foster levy against the clergy (Document 11.3)? Why do you think this address aroused such passion among abolition supporters and opponents? How do Foster's claims that churches are proslavery compare with Garrison's claim that the Constitution is proslavery?

4. What were the demands of the Liberty Party in 1844 (Document 11.4)? How did the party invoke the Constitution to argue for abolition?

5. Why did Frederick Douglass adopt an antislavery interpretation of the Constitution (Document 11.5)? What does he mean by describing slavery as "a system of lawless violence"? How, according to Douglass, could Americans best fight slavery?

PUT IT IN CONTEXT

1. Which abolitionists do you think made the most compelling arguments, and why are these arguments so effective? Can you identify any middle ground where Garrisonians and political abolitionists could agree?

2. How did abolitionism resemble other reform movements of this era in its stance on politics versus moral suasion? How did it differ?

Sectional Politics and the Rise of the Republican Party

Heated debate over slavery's fate in the lands acquired by the United States in the Mexican-American War marked the unraveling of compromise on the peculiar institution. The Compromise of 1850 and the Kansas-Nebraska Act of 1854 only intensified sectional tensions. The nation's political parties reflected these divisions as they rapidly became less "national" in character. By 1854 the Democrats had lost support in the North, but the party remained prominent in the South. The Whig Party collapsed, opening the door for a new political coalition. Some former Whigs joined the American, or Know-Nothing, Party, which found short-term success capitalizing on nativist sentiment. But it was the Republican Party that emerged as the voice of the antislavery North.

Founded in 1854, the Republican Party appealed to antislavery Whigs, including Abraham Lincoln (Document 12.1), and former members of the Free-Soil Party. The Free-Soil Party's calls for "free soil, free labor, and free men" symbolized the desires of most white Northerners to keep western lands free from slavery and therefore open to free white settlement. Republicans expanded on this agenda as they tried to develop a platform (Document 12.2) that would appeal to a majority of the nation. Yet the divide between regional sections and national political parties only widened in the late 1850s. The beating of Senator Charles Sumner after his remarks opposing slavery in Kansas (Document 12.3) intensified sectional rivalries and inspired further action from opponents of slavery, including women like Lydia Maria Child (Document 12.4). By the election of 1860, many Southerners had concluded that they could not remain in the Union if the Republican Abraham Lincoln, who had risen to national prominence opposing slavery during a series of debates with Stephen Douglas (Document 12.5), won the presidency.

The following documents trace the rise of the Republican Party during the 1850s. As you examine these sources, consider the ways that Republicans tried to make their party and their ideals appeal to the widest possible audience.

DOCUMENT 12.1 | ABRAHAM LINCOLN, *On Slavery* (1854)

Abraham Lincoln, the former Whig representative from Illinois, joined the Republican Party shortly after it formed in 1854. Like many other antislavery Whigs, Lincoln believed that American workers could thrive only if slavery ceased to expand. In the following statement, Lincoln argues for the benefits of free labor.

Equality in society alike beats inequality, whether the latter be of the British aristocratic sort or of the domestic slavery sort. We know Southern men declare that their slaves are better off than hired laborers amongst us. How little they know whereof they speak! There is no permanent class of hired laborers amongst us. Twenty-five years ago I was a hired laborer. The hired laborer of yesterday labors on his own account to-day, and will hire others to labor for him to-morrow. Advancement—improvement in condition—is the order of things in a society of equals. As labor is the common burden of our race, so the effort of some to shift their share of the burden onto the shoulders of others is the great durable curse of the race. Originally a curse for transgression upon the whole race, when, as by slavery, it is concentrated on a part only, it becomes the double-refined curse of God upon his creatures.

Free labor has the inspiration of hope; pure slavery has no hope. The power of hope upon human exertion and happiness is wonderful. The slave-master himself has a conception of it, and hence the system of tasks among slaves. The slave whom you cannot drive with the lash to break seventy-five pounds of hemp in a day, if you will task him to break a hundred, and promise him pay for all he does over, he will break you a hundred and fifty. You have substituted hope for the rod. And yet perhaps it does not occur to you that to the extent of your gain in the case, you have given up the slave system and adopted the free system of labor.

Source: John G. Nicolay and John Hay, eds., *Abraham Lincoln: Complete Works, Comprising His Speeches, Letters, State Papers, and Miscellaneous Writings*, vol. 1 (New York: The Century Co., 1907), 179.

DOCUMENT 12.2 | *Republican Party Platform* (1856)

The young Republican Party made an immediate impact in the election of 1856, earning support particularly in the Midwest. The following is an excerpt from the party's 1856 platform, which devoted much of its attention to the debate over the status of Kansas statehood.

This convention of delegates, assembled in pursuance of a call addressed to the people of the United States, without regard to past political differences or divisions, who are opposed to the repeal of the Missouri compromise, to the policy of the

Source: *Official Proceedings of the National Republican Conventions* (Minneapolis: Charles W. Johnson, 1903), 357–59.

present administration, to the extension of slavery into free territory, in favor of admitting Kansas as a free state, of restoring the action of the federal government to the principles of Washington and Jefferson, and who purpose to unite in presenting candidates for the offices of President and Vice-President, do resolve as follows:

1. That the maintenance of the principles promulgated in the Declaration of Independence and embodied in the federal constitution is essential to the preservation of our republican institutions, and that the federal constitution, the rights of the states, and the union of the states, shall be preserved; that, with our republican fathers, we hold it to be a self-evident truth, that all men are endowed with the inalienable rights to life, liberty, and the pursuit of happiness, and that the primary object and ulterior design of our federal government were to secure these rights to all persons within its exclusive jurisdiction; that, as our republican fathers, when they had abolished slavery in all our national territory, ordained that no person shall be deprived of life, liberty, or property without due process of law, it becomes our duty to maintain this provision of the constitution, against all attempts to violate it for the purpose of establishing slavery in the United States, by positive legislation prohibiting its existence or extension therein; that we deny the authority of congress, of a territorial legislature, of any individual or association of individuals to give legal existence to slavery in any territory of the United States while the present Constitution shall be maintained.

2. That the constitution confers upon congress sovereign power over the territories of the United States for their government, and that in the exercise of this power it is both the right and the duty of congress to prohibit in the territories those twin relics of barbarism, — polygamy and slavery.

3. That, while the constitution of the United States was ordained and established by the people "in order to form a more perfect union, establish justice, insure domestic tranquillity, provide for the common defense, promote the general welfare, and secure the blessings of liberty," and contains ample provisions for the protection of the life, liberty, and property of every citizen, the dearest constitutional rights of the people of Kansas have been fraudulently and violently taken from them; their territory has been invaded by an armed force; spurious and pretended legislative, judicial, and executive officers have been set over them, by whose usurped authority, sustained by the military power of the government, tyrannical and unconstitutional laws have been enacted and enforced; the right of the people to keep and bear arms has been infringed; test-oaths of an extraordinary and entangling nature have been imposed as a condition of exercising the right of suffrage and holding office; the right of an accused person to a speedy and public trial by an impartial jury has been denied; the right of the people to be secure in their persons, houses, papers, and effects, against unreasonable searches and seizures, has been violated; they have been deprived of life, liberty, and property without due process of law; the freedom of speech and of the press has been abridged; the right to choose their representatives has been made of no effect; murders, robberies, and arsons have been instigated and encouraged, and the offenders have been allowed

to go unpunished; that all these things have been done with the knowledge, sanction, and procurement of the present administration,—and that for this high crime against the constitution, the Union, and humanity, we arraign that administration, the President, his advisers, agents, supporters, apologists, and accessories, either *before* or *after* the fact, before the country, and before the world; and that it is our fixed purpose to bring the actual perpetrators of these atrocious outrages and their accomplices to a sure and condign punishment thereafter.

4. That Kansas should be immediately admitted as a state of this Union, with her present free constitution, as at once the most effectual way of securing to her citizens the enjoyment of the rights and privileges to which they are entitled, and of ending the civil strife now raging in her territory.

5. That the highwayman's plea, that "might makes right," embodied in the Ostend circular, was in every respect unworthy of American diplomacy, and would bring shame and dishonor upon any government or people that gave it their sanction.

6. That a railroad to the Pacific ocean by the most central and practicable route is imperatively demanded by the interests of the whole country, and that the federal government ought to render immediate and efficient aid in its construction; and, as an auxiliary thereto, to the immediate construction of an emigrant route on the line of the railroad.

7. That appropriations by congress for the improvement of rivers and harbors of a national character, required for the accommodation and security of our existing commerce, are authorized by the constitution and justified by the obligation of government to protect the lives and property of its citizens.

8. That we invite the affiliation and co-operation of freemen of all parties, however differing from us in other respects, in support of the principles herein declared; and, believing that the spirit of our institutions, as well as the constitution of our country, guarantees liberty of conscience and equality of rights among citizens, we oppose all legislation impairing their security.

DOCUMENT 12.3 | CHARLES SUMNER, *The Crime against Kansas* (1856)

Senator Charles Sumner of Massachusetts, who quickly became one of the key leaders of the Republican Party, spoke out in Congress against the expansion of slavery into Kansas. In the following excerpt, Sumner directs his anger toward South Carolina senator Andrew Butler. Butler's nephew, South Carolina representative Preston Brooks, retaliated by caning Sumner until he was bloody and unconscious.

Source: Charles Sumner, *The Crime against Kansas, the Apologies for the Crime, the True Remedy* (Boston: John P. Jewett and Company, 1856), 9–11.

But, before entering upon the argument, I must say something of a general character, particularly in response to what has fallen from senators who have raised themselves to eminence on this floor in championship of human wrongs; I mean the senator from South Carolina [Mr. BUTLER], and the senator from Illinois [Mr. DOUGLAS], who, though unlike as Don Quixote and Sancho Panza, yet, like this couple, sally forth together in the same adventure. I regret much to miss the elder senator from his seat; but the cause against which he has run a tilt with such activity of animosity demands that the opportunity of exposing him should not be lost; and it is for the cause that I speak. The senator from South Carolina has read many books of chivalry, and believes himself a chivalrous knight, with sentiments of honor and courage. Of course he has chosen a mistress to whom he has made his vows, and who, though ugly to others, is always lovely to him; though polluted in the sight of the world, is chaste in his sight;—I mean the harlot Slavery. For her his tongue is always profuse with words. Let her be impeached in character, or any proposition made to shut her out from the extension of her wantonness, and no extravagance of manner or hardihood of assertion is then too great for this senator. The frenzy of Don Quixote in behalf of his wench Dulcinea del Toboso is all surpassed. The asserted rights of Slavery, which shock equality of all kinds, are cloaked by a fantastic claim of equality. If the slave States cannot enjoy what, in mockery of the great fathers of the Republic, he misnames equality under the Constitution,—in other words, the full power in the National Territories to compel fellow-men to unpaid toil, to separate husband and wife, and to sell little children at the auction-block,—then, sir, the chivalric senator will conduct the State of South Carolina out of the Union! Heroic knight! Exalted senator! A Second Moses come for a second exodus!

But, not content with this poor menace, which we have been twice told was "measured," the senator, in the unrestrained chivalry of his nature, has undertaken to apply opprobrious words to those who differ from him on this floor. He calls them "sectional and fanatical;" and opposition to the usurpation in Kansas he denounces as "uncalculating fanaticism." To be sure, these charges lack all grace of originality, and all sentiment of truth; but the adventurous senator does not hesitate. He is the uncompromising, unblushing representative on this floor of a flagrant *sectionalism*, which now domineers over the Republic; and yet, with a ludicrous ignorance of his own position,—unable to see himself as others see him,—or with an effrontery which even his white head ought not to protect from rebuke, he applies to those here who resist his *sectionalism* the very epithet which designates himself. The men who strive to bring back the government to its original policy, when Freedom and not Slavery was national, while Slavery and not Freedom was sectional, he arraigns as *sectional*. This will not do. It involves too great a perversion of terms. I tell that senator that it is to himself, and to the "organization" of which he is the "committed advocate," that this epithet belongs. I now fasten it upon them. For myself, I care little for names; but, since the question has been raised here, I affirm that the Republican party of the Union is in no just sense *sectional*, but, more than any other party, *national*; and that it now goes forth to dislodge from the high places of the government the tyrannical sectionalism of which the senator from South Carolina is one of the maddest zealots.

To the charge of fanaticism I also reply. Sir, fanaticism is found in an enthusiasm or exaggeration of opinions, particularly on religious subjects; but there may be a fanaticism for evil as well as for good. Now, I will not deny that there are persons among us loving Liberty too well for their personal good, in a selfish generation. Such there may be, and, for the sake of their example, would that there were more! In calling them "fanatics," you cast contumely upon the noble army of martyrs, from the earliest day down to this hour; upon the great tribunes of human rights, by whom life, liberty, and happiness on earth, have been secured; upon the long line of devoted patriots, who, throughout history, have truly loved their country; and upon all, who, in noble aspirations for the general good, and in forgetfulness of self, have stood out before their age, and gathered into their generous bosoms the shafts of tyranny and wrong, in order to make a pathway for truth.

DOCUMENT 12.4 | LYDIA MARIA CHILD, *Letters to Mrs. S. B. Shaw and Miss Lucy Osgood* (1856)

After Preston Brooks's attack on Charles Sumner, "Bleeding Sumner" joined "Bleeding Kansas" as a rallying cry for abolitionists, including the prolific author Lydia Maria Child of Massachusetts. In the following letters, Child expresses her support for Republican presidential candidate John C. Frémont and reveals her thoughts on the Sumner attack, women's rights, and sectional politics. In doing so, she offers a prophetic view of the years to come.

To Mrs. S. B. Shaw, Wayland, 1856. [no month/date given]

The outrage upon Charles Sumner made me literally ill for several days. It brought on nervous headache and painful suffocations about the heart. If I could only have done something, it would have loosened that tight ligature that seemed to stop the flowing of my blood. But I never was one who knew how to serve the Lord by standing and waiting; and to stand and wait then! It almost drove me mad. And that miserable Faneuil Hall meeting! The time-serving Mr.— talking about his "friend" Sumner's being a man that "hit hard!" making the people laugh at his own witticisms, when a volcano was seething beneath their feet! poisoning the well-spring of popular indignation, which was rising in its might! Mr. A., on the eve of departing for Europe, wrote to me, "The North will not really do anything to maintain their own dignity. See if they do! I am willing to go abroad, to find some relief from the mental pain that the course of public affairs in this country has for many years caused me." But I am more hopeful. Such a man as Charles Sumner will not bleed and suffer in vain. Those noble martyrs of liberty in Kansas will prove missionary ghosts, walking through the land, rousing the nation from its guilty slumbers. Our hopes, like yours, rest on Fremont. I would almost lay down my life to have him elected. There never has been such a crisis since we were a nation. If the slave-power is checked now, it will never regain its strength. If it is not checked, civil war is inevitable; and, with all my horror of bloodshed, I could be better resigned to that great calamity than to endure the

Source: *Letters of Lydia Maria Child* (Boston: Houghton Mifflin, 1882), 78–80.

tyranny that has so long trampled on us. I do believe the North will not, this time, fall asleep again, after shaking her mane and growling a little.

I saw by the papers that Mr. Curtis[1] was in the field, and I rejoiced to know he was devoting his brilliant talents and generous sympathies to so noble a purpose. I envy him; I want to mount the rostrum myself. I have such a fire burning in my soul, that it seems to me I could pour forth a stream of lava that would bury all the respectable servilities, and all the mob servilities, as deep as Pompeii; so that it would be an enormous labor ever to dig up the skeletons of their memories.

We also talk of little else but Kansas and Fremont. What a shame the women can't vote! We'd carry our "Jessie"[2] into the White House on our shoulders; wouldn't we? Never mind! Wait a while! Woman stock is rising in the market. I shall not live to see women vote; but I'll come and rap at the ballot-box. Won't you? I never was bitten by politics before; but such mighty issues are depending on this election that I cannot be indifferent.

To Miss Lucy Osgood, Wayland, July 9, 1856.

I did not intend to leave your New York letter so long unanswered, but the fact is, recent events have made me heart-sick. My anxiety about Charles Sumner and about the sufferers in Kansas has thrown a pall over everything. The fire of indignation is the only thing that has lighted up my gloom. At times my peace principles have shivered in the wind; and nothing could satisfy my mood but Jeanne d'arc's floating banner and consecrated sword. And when this state of mind was rebuked by the remembrance of him who taught us to overcome evil only with good, I could do nothing better than groan out, in a tone of despairing reproach, "How long, O Lord! How long?" Certainly there are gleams of light amid the darkness. There has been more spirit roused in the North than I thought was in her. I begin to hope that either the slave power must yield to argument and the majesty of public sentiment or else that we shall see an army in the field, stout and unyielding as Cromwell's band.

DOCUMENT 12.5 | *The Lincoln-Douglas Debates* (1858)

In 1858 the Republican Party nominated Abraham Lincoln to challenge incumbent Democratic Illinois senator Stephen Douglas. Douglas won the election, but the contest established Lincoln as a potential Republican candidate for the presidency. The campaign featured a series of seven debates, in which the candidates tackled the most important subjects of the day: slavery, free labor, and black citizenship following the *Dred Scott* decision. The following excerpt comes from the second debate, held in Freeport, Illinois.

Source: Alonzo T. Jones, ed., *Political Speeches and Debates of Abraham Lincoln and Stephen A. Douglas, 1854–1861* (Battle Creek, MI: International Tract Society, 1895), 202–3, 217–18.

[1]**Mr. Curtis**: George William Curtis, Republican writer and orator who campaigned for Frémont.

[2]**"Jessie"**: Jessie Benton Frémont, writer and wife of John C. Frémont.

[Mr. Lincoln] I am rather disposed to take up at least some of these questions, and state what I really think upon them.

As to the first one, in regard to the Fugitive-Slave law, I have never hesitated to say, and I do not now hesitate to say, that I think, under the Constitution of the United States, the people of the Southern States are entitled to a Congressional Fugitive-Slave law. Having said that, I have had nothing to say in regard to the existing Fugitive-Slave law, further than that I think it should have been framed so as to be free from some of the objections that pertain to it, without lessening its efficiency. And inasmuch as we are not now in an agitation in regard to an alteration or modification of that law, I would not be the man to introduce it as a new subject of agitation upon the general question of slavery.

In regard to the other question, of whether I am pledged to the admission of any more Slave States into the Union, I state to you very frankly that I would be exceedingly sorry ever to be put in a position of having to pass upon that question. I should be exceedingly glad to know that there would never be another Slave State admitted into the Union; but I must add that if slavery shall be kept out of the Territories during the Territorial existence of any one given Territory, and then the people shall, having a fair chance and a clear field, when they come to adopt the constitution, do such an extraordinary thing as to adopt a slave constitution, uninfluenced by the actual presence of the institution among them, I see no alternative, if we own the country, but to admit them into the Union. . . .

The fourth one is in regard to the abolition of slavery in the District of Columbia. In relation to that, I have my mind very distinctly made up. I should be exceedingly glad to see slavery abolished in the District of Columbia. I believe that Congress possesses the constitutional power to abolish it. Yet as a member of Congress, I should not, with my present views, be in favor of *endeavoring* to abolish slavery in the District of Columbia, unless it would be upon these conditions: *First*, that the abolition should be gradual; *second*, that it should be on a vote of the majority of qualified voters in the District; and *third*, that compensation should be made to unwilling owners. . . .

[Mr. Douglas] I trust now that Mr. Lincoln will deem himself answered on his four points. He racked his brain so much in devising these four questions that he exhausted himself, and had not strength enough to invent the others. As soon as he is able to hold a council with his advisers, Lovejoy, Farnsworth, and Fred Douglass, he will frame and propound others. [Voices: "Good, good."] You Black Republicans who say good, I have no doubt think that they are all good men.

I have reason to recollect that some people in this country think that Fred Douglass is a very good man. The last time I came here to make a speech, while talking from the stand to you, people of Freeport, as I am doing to-day, I saw a carriage—and a magnificent one it was,—drive up and take a position on the outside of the crowd; a beautiful young lady was sitting on the box-seat, whilst Fred Douglass and her mother reclined inside, and the owner of the carriage acted as driver. I saw this in your own town. [Voices: "What of it?"] All I have to say of it is this, that if you, Black Republicans, think that the negro ought to be on a social equality with your wives and daughters, and ride in a carriage with your wife, whilst you drive the team, you have perfect right to do so.

I am told that one of Fred Douglass's kinsmen, another rich black negro, is now traveling in this part of the State, making speeches for his friend Lincoln as the champion of black men. [Voices: "What have you to say against it?"] All I have to say on that subject is, that those of you who believe that the negro is your equal and ought to be on an equality with you socially, politically, and legally, have a right to entertain those opinions, and of course will vote for Mr. Lincoln.

INTERPRET THE EVIDENCE

1. According to Abraham Lincoln, what are the benefits of a free-labor system over a system of slavery (Document 12.1)? How does Lincoln use his own life story as evidence?

2. How did the Republican Party platform of 1856 address the issue of Kansas statehood (Document 12.2)? Why do you think it also included resolutions regarding internal improvements?

3. What are Charles Sumner's criticisms of Andrew Butler and of the institution of slavery (Document 12.3)? How does he defend himself from claims that he is the fanatical head of a sectional party?

4. How did "Bleeding Kansas" and the beating of Charles Sumner influence the politics of Lydia Maria Child (Document 12.4)? What kind of abolitionism did Child endorse? What roles did she believe women should play in politics?

5. What are Lincoln's arguments regarding the future of slavery and the fugitive slave law (Document 12.5)? Does he call for abolition? How does Stephen Douglas attempt to characterize Lincoln? Why does he seek to tie Lincoln to Frederick Douglass and issues of racial equality?

PUT IT IN CONTEXT

1. According to the individuals featured in these documents, who is responsible for ending slavery? What role do they envision the Republican Party playing in ending the peculiar institution? How do these documents show how abolitionism had evolved over time?

2. In what ways do these prominent Republicans call for an end to slavery without necessarily calling for black equality? How have they expanded the Free-Soil Party platform to appeal to a wider constituency?

Home-Front Protest during the Civil War

The Civil War aroused considerable dissent on the home front. In the North, criticism came from many sides. Many whites resented fighting what they saw as a war to free blacks, who they believed would move to the North and drive down wages. The passage of a conscription law in 1863 drove whites in a number of cities, most notably New York, to violence (Document 13.2). Democrats tried to take political advantage of the antiwar impulse, arguing that President Lincoln and his party were waging a war that produced a catastrophic casualty rate and would ultimately do far more harm than good. Democrats who opposed the war, known by their opponents as Copperheads, found a receptive audience in many parts of the North. Ohio congressman Clement L. Vallandigham (Document 13.3) became their chief spokesman.

The northern working classes and the poor saw few economic benefits from the war, and Northerners generally suffered from rising prices. But Southerners suffered from even worse inflation, and by 1863 civilians had to deal as well with shortages of food, clothing, and other necessities of life. In the South, white women took the lead in protesting the scarcities created by the war, highlighted by the Richmond Bread Riot of 1863 (Document 13.1). As in the North, Southerners bristled at the Confederate draft law, which seemed to contradict the region's professed ideal of each state's right to self-government. Many angry Confederates even called for peace (Document 13.4), although these peace advocates proposed only limited concessions to the North in order to reunite the nation. As casualties mounted, many Southerners, including Confederate women (Document 13.5), began to wonder whether the war was worth it.

The following documents offer examples of the dissent expressed throughout the nation during the war years. As you read these sources, consider how the Civil War penetrated every aspect of Northerners' and Southerners' lives and shaped their politics.

DOCUMENT 13.1 | JOHN BEAUCHAMP JONES, *The Richmond Bread Riot* (1866)

On April 2, 1863, angry and hungry women led a protest march through downtown Richmond, Virginia. As the mob grew, so did its pillaging, as marchers ransacked stores for food and other items. Virginia governor John L. Letcher and Confederate president Jefferson Davis arrived on the scene, and the crowd eventually dispersed. As a clerk in the Confederate war department stationed in Richmond, John Beauchamp Jones observed the Richmond bread riot firsthand.

April 2nd. — This morning early a few hundred women and boys met as by concert in the Capitol Square, saying they were hungry, and must have food. The number continued to swell until there were more than a thousand. But few men were among them, and these were mostly foreign residents, with exemptions in their pockets. About nine A.M. the mob emerged from the western gates of the square, and proceeded down Ninth Street, passing the War Department, and crossing Main Street, increasing in magnitude at every step, but preserving silence and (so far) good order. Not knowing the meaning of such a procession, I asked a pale boy where they were going. A young woman, seemingly emaciated, but yet with a smile, answered that they were going to find something to eat. I could not, for the life of me, refrain from expressing the hope that they might be successful; and I remarked they were going in the right direction to find plenty in the hands of the extortioners. I did not follow, to see what they did; but I learned an hour after that they marched through Cary Street, and entered diverse stores of the speculators, which they proceeded to empty of their contents. They impressed all the carts and drays [wagons] in the street, which were speedily laden with meal, flour, shoes, etc. I did not learn whither these were driven; but probably they were rescued from those in charge of them. Nevertheless, an immense amount of provisions, and other articles, were borne by the mob, which continued to increase in numbers. An eye-witness says he saw a boy come out of a store with a hat full of money (notes); and I learned that when the mob turned up into Main Street, when all the shops were by this time closed, they broke in the plate-glass windows, demanding silks, jewelry, etc. Here they were incited to pillage valuables, not necessary for subsistence, by the class of residents (aliens) exempted from military duty by Judge Campbell, Assistant Secretary of War, in contravention of Judge Meredith's decision. Thus the work of spoliation went on, until the military appeared upon the scene, summoned by Gov. Letcher, whose term of service is near its close. He had the Riot Act read (by the mayor), and then threatened to fire on the mob. He gave them five minutes' time to disperse in, threatening to use military force (the city battalion being present) if they did not comply with the demand. The timid women fell back, and a pause was put

Source: J. B. Jones, *A Rebel War Clerk's Diary at the Confederate States Capital* (Philadelphia: J. B. Lippincott & Co., 1866), 284–86.

to the devastation, though but few believed he would venture to put his threat in execution. If he had done so, he would have been hung, no doubt.

About this time the President appeared, and ascending a dray [wagon], spoke to the people. He urged them to return to their homes, so that the bayonets there menacing them might be sent against the common enemy. He told them that such acts would bring famine upon them in the only form which could not be provided against, as it would deter people from bringing food to the city. He said he was willing to share his last loaf with the suffering people (his best horse had been stolen the night before), and he trusted we would all bear our privations with fortitude, and continue united against the Northern invaders, who were the authors of all our sufferings. He seemed deeply moved; and indeed it was a frightful spectacle, and perhaps an ominous one, if the government does not remove some of the quartermasters who have contributed very much to bring about the evil of scarcity. I mean those who have allowed transportation to forestallers [shops not licensed to receive these goods] and extortioners.

Gen. Elzey and Gen. Winder waited upon the Secretary of War in the morning, asking permission to call the troops from the camps near the city, to suppress the women and children by a summary process. But Mr. Seddon hesitated, and then declined authorizing any such absurdity. He said it was a municipal or State duty, and therefore he would not take the responsibility of interfering in the matter. Even in the moment of aspen consternation, he was still the politician.

I have not heard of any injuries sustained by the women and children. Nor have I heard how many stores the mob visited; and it must have been many.

All is quiet now (three P.M.); and I understand the government is issuing rice to the people.

DOCUMENT 13.2 | *Testimony of New York City Draft Riot Victim Mrs. Statts, Collected by the Committee of Merchants for the Relief of Colored People, Suffering from the Late Riots* (1863)

The Enrollment Act, which authorized conscription in the North, outraged many working-class city dwellers. In New York City, whites—including native-born whites and Irish and German immigrants—rioted for four days in July 1863. At least 120 people died, and 11 black men were lynched by the mob. In the following testimony, collected by a group of merchants who investigated the riots, an African American woman named Mrs. Statts provides a firsthand account of the violence.

Source: *Report of the Committee of Merchants for the Relief of Colored People, Suffering from the Late Riots in the City of New York* (New York: George A. Whitehorne, 1863).

At 3 o'clock of that day the mob arrived and immediately commenced an attack with terrific yells, and a shower of stones and bricks, upon the house. In the next room to where I was sitting was a poor woman, who had been confined with a child on Sunday, three days previous. Some of the rioters broke through the front door with pickaxes, and came rushing into the room where this poor woman lay, and commenced to pull the clothes from off her. Knowing that their rage was chiefly directed against men, I hid my son behind me and ran with him through the back door, down the basement. In a little while I saw the innocent babe, of three days old, come crashing down into the yard; some of the rioters had dashed it out of the back window, killing it instantly. In a few minutes streams of water came pouring down into the basement, the mob had cut the Croton water-pipes with their axes. Fearing we should be drowned in the cellar, (there were ten of us, mostly women and children, there) I took my boy and flew past the dead body of the babe, out to the rear of the yard, hoping to escape with him through an open lot into Twenty-ninth-street; but here, to our horror and dismay, we met the mob again; I, with my son, had climbed the fence, but the sight of those maddened demons so affected me that I fell back, fainting, into the yard; my son jumped down from the fence to pick me up, and a dozen of the rioters came leaping over the fence after him. As they surrounded us, my son exclaimed, "Save my mother; gentlemen, if you kill me." "Well, we will kill you," they answered; and with that two ruffians seized him, each taking hold of an arm, while a third, armed with a crow-bar, calling upon them to stand and hold his arms apart, deliberately struck him a heavy blow over the head, felling him, like a bullock, to the ground. (He died in the New-York Hospital two days after.) I believe if I were to live a hundred years I would never forget that scene, or cease to hear the horrid voices of that demoniacal mob resounding in my ears.

They then drove me over the fence, and as I was passing over one of the mob seized a pocket-book, which he saw in my bosom, and in his eagerness to get it tore the dress off my shoulders.

I, with several others, then ran to the Twenty-ninth-street Station-house, but we were here refused admittance, and told by the Captain that we were frightened without cause. A gentleman accompanied us who told the Captain of the facts, but we were all turned away.

I then went down to my husband's, in Broome-street, and there I encountered another mob, who, before I could escape, commenced stoning me. They beat me severely.

I reached the house but found my husband had left for Rahway. Scarcely knowing what I did, I then wandered, bewildered and sick, in the direction he had taken, and toward Philadelphia, and reached Jersey City, where a kind, Christian gentleman, Mr. ARTHUR LYNCH, found me and took me to his house, where his good wife nursed me for over two weeks, While I was very sick.

I am a member of the Baptist Church, and if it were not for my trust in Christ I do not know how I could have endured it.

DOCUMENT 13.3 | CLEMENT L. VALLANDIGHAM, *The Civil War in America* (1863)

Ohio representative Clement L. Vallandigham led the Copperhead faction of the Democratic Party in its opposition to the Civil War. In May 1863 he was arrested on treason charges after making a speech against the Lincoln administration. A military court sentenced him to prison, but President Lincoln instead banished him to the Confederacy. Soon after, Vallandigham fled to Canada, where he mounted a failed campaign to become governor of Ohio. Vallandigham spoke before the House of Representatives in January 1863, just a few months before his arrest.

And now, sir, I recur to the state of the Union to-day. What is it? Sir, twenty months have elapsed, but the rebellion is not crushed out; its military power has not been broken; the insurgents have not dispersed. The Union is not restored; nor the Constitution maintained; nor the laws enforced. Twenty, sixty, ninety, three hundred, six hundred days have passed; a thousand millions been expended; and three hundred thousand lives lost or bodies mangled; and to-day the Confederate flag is still near the Potomac and the Ohio, and the Confederate Government stronger, many times, than at the beginning. Not a State has been restored, not any part of any State has voluntarily returned to the Union. And has any thing been wanting that Congress, or the States, or the people in their most generous enthusiasm, their most impassionate patriotism, could bestow? Was it power? And did not the party of the Executive control the entire Federal Government, every State Government, every county, every city, town, and village in the North and West? Was it patronage? All belonged to it. Was it influence? What more? Did not the school, the college, the church, the press, the secret orders, the municipality, the corporation, railroads, telegraphs, express companies, the voluntary association, all, all yield it to the utmost? Was it unanimity? Never was an Administration so supported in England or America. Five men and half a score of newspapers made up the Opposition. Was it enthusiasm? The enthusiasm was fanatical. There has been nothing like it since the Crusades. Was it confidence? Sir, the faith of the people exceeded that of the patriarch. They gave up Constitution, law, right, liberty, all at your demand for arbitrary power that the rebellion might, as you promised, be crushed out in three months, and the Union restored. Was credit needed? You took control of a country, young, vigorous, and inexhaustible in wealth and resources, and of a Government almost free from public debt, and whose good faith had never been tarnished. . . . A thousand millions have been expended since the 15th of April, 1861; and a public debt or liability of $1,500,000,000 already incurred. And to support all this stupendous outlay and indebtedness, a system of taxation, direct and indirect, has been inaugurated, the most onerous and unjust ever imposed upon any but a conquered people.

Money and credit, then, you have had in prodigal profusion. And were men wanted? More than a million rushed to arms! Seventy-five thousand first (and the country stood aghast at the multitude), then eighty-three thousand more

Source: *Speeches, Arguments, Addresses, and Letters of Clement L. Vallandigham* (New York: J. Walter & Co., 1864), 427–29, 439–40.

were demanded; and three hundred and ten thousand responded to the call. The President next asked for four hundred thousand, and Congress, in their generous confidence, gave him five hundred thousand; and, not to be outdone, he took six hundred and thirty-seven thousand. Half of these melted away in their first campaign; and the President demanded three hundred thousand more for the war, and then drafted yet another three hundred thousand for nine months. The fabled hosts of Xerxes have been outnumbered. And yet victory, strangely, follows the standard of the foe. From Great Bethel to Vicksburg, the battle has not been to the strong. Yet every disaster, except the last, has been followed by a call for more troops, and every time, so far, they have been promptly furnished. From the beginning the war has been conducted like a political campaign, and it has been the folly of the party in power that they have assumed, that numbers alone would win the field in a contest not with ballots but with musket and sword. . . .

Then, sir, there is not an "irrepressible conflict" between slave labor and free labor. There is no conflict at all. Both exist together in perfect harmony in the South. The master and the slave, the white laborer and the black, work together in the same field, or the same shop, and without the slightest sense of degradation. They are not equals, either socially or politically. And why, then, cannot Ohio, having only free labor, live in harmony with Kentucky, which has both slave and free? Above all, why cannot Massachusetts allow the same right of choice to South Carolina, separated as they are a thousand miles, by other States, who would keep the peace, and live in good-will? Why this civil war? Whence disunion? Not from slavery—not because the South chooses to have two kinds of labor instead of one—but from *sectionalism*, always and everywhere a disintegrating principle. Sectional jealousy and hate—these, sir, are the only elements of conflict between these States; and, though powerful, they are yet not at all irrepressible.

DOCUMENT 13.4 | *Calls for Peace in North Carolina* (1863)

As the war dragged on in the South, some Southerners believed it made more sense to attempt peace negotiations than to continue a bloody, costly conflict. When the Confederates lost the Battle of Antietam and Confederate general Robert E. Lee withdrew from Maryland in 1862, the fledgling peace movement gained adherents. The following account of a North Carolina peace movement meeting appeared in the Raleigh *North Carolina Standard* in August 1863.

Public Meeting in Wake County

At a meeting of the people of Little River district, Wake County, held at Rosenburg on the 24th July, on motion of B. T. Strickland, Dr. G. M. Cooley was called to the chair, and Harrington Daniel was appointed Secretary. On motion, B. T. Strickland, A. R. Horton, and H. Daniel were appointed a committee to report resolutions. The committee soon after reported the following resolutions through their chairman, which were unanimously adopted:

Source: *North Carolina Standard (Raleigh)*, August 5, 1863.

Whereas, The time has arrived when people of North-Carolina should watch their own rights and interests with a jealous eye; and Whereas we, a portion of the people, have thought proper to meet together to express our views in relation to the policy pursued towards this State by the Confederate government, and to take a position in defense of our liberties . . . against kings abroad or tyrants at home. Therefore—

Resolved, That the course of the administration at Richmond towards North-Carolina has been any thing but fair. While she has put more men in the field than any other State according to population, and while her sons have every where fought and charged the enemy with unsurpassed courage, she receives but little credit for valor or patriotism, and has fewer Generals than any other State to command her troops. Our people have long complained of this injustice, but thus far their complaints have been disregarded.

Resolved, That North Carolina has men as well qualified to examine and enrol[l] her conscripts as can be sent here from the City of Richmond; and the course pursued in this respect towards the State is an insult to the intelligence of her people. . . .

Resolved, That the President having called upon the Governor of the State for more troops, we deem the call unjust until other States have furnished their quota. . . .

Resolved, That it is a great crime . . . to conceal the truth from the people. From the beginning of this war until the present the enemy has gained slowly but surely upon us, and but for the extraordinary courage of our troops, their flag would long since have floated from all our capitols.

Resolved, That we favor a proposition of peace to the enemy upon such terms as will guarantee to us all our rights upon an equality with the North; and if such a proposition should be made to and rejected by them, we would be willing to die to the last man upon the battle-field in defense of those rights and that equality. We feel that it is time to consult reason and common sense, and to discard prejudice and passion. The people must look and act upon things as they are.

Resolved, That peace cannot be reached merely by fighting. This, we think, is now apparent to all. The birth of a nation is a great event, and so is the decay and death of a nation. Unless Providence should smile upon us—and see no indication that He will—the war will go on until one side or the other shall conquer.

DOCUMENT 13.5 | ELLA GERTRUDE CLANTON THOMAS, *Diary* (1864)

Wealthy Confederate women, who took on new responsibilities as their husbands served as soldiers or in politics, felt acutely the mounting costs of the war. Although they did not protest publicly, many Confederate women came to question the war effort. Ella Gertrude Clanton Thomas, a college-educated elite woman from Augusta, Georgia, recorded her evolving thoughts on the war in her diary.

Source: Ella Gertrude Clanton Thomas, *Secret Eye: The Journal of Ella Gertrude Clanton Thomas, 1848–1889* (Chapel Hill: University of North Carolina Press, 1990).

November 17, 1864: . . . This is a dark hour in our country's history. Lincoln has been elected by 300,000 majority and Northern papers say that Sherman is preparing for a winter campaign through the cotton states with five corps, leaving a sufficient force to hold Chattanooga and look after Hood. Sherman some years ago was stationed at the arsenal 1 at the Sand Hills and has been the recipient of hospitality from numerous citizens of this place. President Davis in his message says that we are better off than we were this time last year, but when President Davis advocates the training of Negroes to aid us in fighting — promising them, as an inducement to do so, their freedom, and in the same message intimates that rather than yield we would place every Negro in the Army — he so clearly betrays the weakness of our force that I candidly confess I am disheartened. I take a woman's view of the subject but it does seem strangely inconsistent, the idea of our offering to a Negro the rich boon — the priceless reward of freedom to aid us in keeping in bondage a large portion of his brethren, when by joining the Yankees he will instantly gain the very reward which Mr Davis offers to him after a certain amount of labor rendered and danger incurred. Mr Davis to the contrary, the Negro has had a great deal to do with this war and if — but I fear I grow toryish in my sentiments —

Monday, November 21, 1864: Oh God will this war never cease? Will we ever settle quietly in our old peaceful domestic relations? How strange it all seems. Even now I can scarcely realize the state of suspense in which we have all been placed during the past few days. I don't believe I have felt so gloomy at anytime tho as I did Saturday afternoon. During the morning I rode out (Friday), and just as I was leaving the house I received a letter from Mr Thomas written the Sunday previous — Said he "Ah you can form no idea how much I miss you — good bye to you and all my little ones." . . .

Short as the time has been since Thursday, I can scarcely collect the link of events sufficiently to tell how the time has been spent. Oh I remember now that Mr Scales spent Friday night with us. He was taking a gloomy view of our prospects, but he talked just this way I remember one year ago. Then I confess I felt more determined "to do and dare and die" than I do now. Saturday we were busy hauling wood from the depot, Mr Selkirk the agent having been good enough to let me have two car loads brought up. It was fortunate I received it when I did as the trains are occupied now in removing government stores to the exclusion of everything else. It was, as yesterday and today have been, dull gloomy days. The whole heavens overcast with clouds — All nature appearing to mourn over the wretched degeneracy of her children and weeping to see brothers arrayed in hatred against each other. "Man, the noblest work of God." Verily, when I witness and read of the track of desolation which Sherman's army leaves behind them, I am constrained to think that the work reflects little credit upon the creator. I know that sounds irreverent but I sigh for the memory of those days when man's noblest, better nature was displayed, when the brute "the cloven foot," was concealed and I could dream and believe that ours was the very best land — ruled by the very best men under the sun!! . . .

INTERPRET THE EVIDENCE

1. How does John Beauchamp Jones describe the participants in the Richmond bread protest (Document 13.1)? What did Beauchamp report that the protesters took? How did Jefferson Davis attempt to stop the riot?

2. How did Mrs. Statts (Document 13.2) describe the New York City draft riots? How does she depict the rioters and the police? What could Statts and other victims do to protect themselves from the rioters? Why did the white protesters target African Americans?

3. Why did Clement L. Vallandigham disagree with the U.S. government's decision to continue the war (Document 13.3)? How did he characterize the war's progress?

4. Why did the North Carolina peace advocates argue against continuing the war (Document 13.4)? What did they hope to gain in a settlement? Do you think their demands were realistic? Why or why not?

5. How had the realities of the war changed Ella Gertrude Clanton Thomas's (Document 13.5) outlook on the Confederate effort? Had she come to sympathize with the Union? Why did she view the idea of arming slaves as problematic?

PUT IT IN CONTEXT

1. How did the Americans represented in this set of documents express their opposition to the war and its consequences? What did the protesters and dissenters have in common? How did their causes and beliefs differ? What were the ramifications of opposition to the war or protest against the war?

2. How did the individuals portrayed in these documents balance personal interests and wartime goals? How might personal goals—of protesters and politicians, of citizens in the North and in the South—have influenced the trajectory of the war?

14

Reconstruction in South Carolina

South Carolina offers an interesting case study of the course of Reconstruction in the South following the Civil War. It was the first state to secede from the Union in 1860, and the majority of its population was black. By the war's end, blacks in South Carolina had already begun what the historian Willie Lee Rose called a "rehearsal for Reconstruction" by occupying the Sea Islands. Once the state reentered the Union, Republican voters elected black officials and even sent African American representatives to serve in Congress. It was the only state where blacks controlled the state legislature.

However, like the other southern states, South Carolina capitulated to white supremacy. The Ku Klux Klan maintained a campaign of terror, and northern support for Reconstruction withered. Commentators like the artist Thomas Nast argued that African American elected officials were unfit for office. The federal government backed away from supporting reconstructed Republican governments, and white Democrats returned to power in South Carolina in 1877. Still, Reconstruction marked a significant, if short-lived, historical moment when African Americans participated in and led an interracial democracy.

The following documents offer an overview of key themes concerning Reconstruction in South Carolina. Consider how people with varied interests—African Americans, northern Republicans, and officials of the federal government—viewed Reconstruction in different, changing ways.

DOCUMENT 14.1 | COLORED PEOPLE'S CONVENTION OF SOUTH CAROLINA, *Memorial to Congress* (1865)

After the Civil War, African Americans in South Carolina wasted no time in asserting their newfound rights as freedpeople. The Colored People's Convention of South Carolina met in November 1865 and presented the following list of demands to Congress.

Source: James S. Allen, *Reconstruction: The Battle for Democracy, 1865–1876* (International Publishers, 1937), Appendix, 228–29.

Gentlemen:

We, the colored people of the State of South Carolina, in Convention assembled, respectfully present for your attention some prominent facts in relation to our present condition, and make a modest yet earnest appeal to your considerate judgment.

We, your memorialists, with profound gratitude to almighty God, recognize the great boon of freedom conferred upon us by the instrumentality of our late President, Abraham Lincoln, and the armies of the United States.

"The fixed decree, which not till Heaven can move,
Thou, Fate, fulfill it; and, ye Powers, approve."

We also recognize with liveliest gratitude the vast services of the Freedmen's Bureau together with the efforts of the good and wise throughout the land to raise up an oppressed and deeply injured people in the scale of civilized being, during the throbbings of a mighty revolution which must affect the future destiny of the world.

Conscious of the difficulties that surround our position, we would ask for no rights or privileges but such as rest upon the strong basis of justice and expediency, in view of the best interests of our entire country.

We ask first, that the strong arm of law and order be placed alike over the entire people of this State; that life and property be secured, and the laborer free to sell his labor as the merchant his goods.

We ask that a fair and impartial instruction be given to the pledges of the government to us concerning the land question.

We ask that the three great agents of civilized society—the school, the pulpit, the press—be as secure in South Carolina as in Massachusetts or Vermont.

We ask that equal suffrage be conferred upon us, in common with the white men of this State.

This we ask, because "all free governments derive their just powers from the consent of the governed"; and we are largely in the majority in this State, bearing for a long period the burden of onerous taxation, without a just representation. We ask for equal suffrage as a protection for the hostility evoked by our known faithfulness to our country and flag under all circumstances.

We ask that colored men shall not in every instance be tried by white men; and that neither by custom or enactment shall we be excluded from the jury box.

We ask that, inasmuch as the Constitution of the United States explicitly declares that the right to keep and bear arms shall not be infringed and the Constitution is the Supreme law of the land—that the late efforts of the Legislature of this State to pass an act to deprive us of arms be forbidden, as a plain violation of the Constitution, and unjust to many of us in the highest degree, who have been soldiers, and purchased our muskets from the United States Government when mustered out of service.

We protest against any code of black laws the Legislature of this State may enact, and pray to be governed by the same laws that control other men. The right to assemble in peaceful convention, to discuss the political questions of the day; the right to enter upon all the avenues of agriculture, commerce, trade; to amass wealth by thrift and industry; the right to develop our whole being by all the appliances that belong to civilized society, cannot be questioned by any class of intelligent legislators.

We solemnly affirm and desire to live orderly and peacefully with all the people of this State; and commending this memorial to your considerate judgment.

Thus we ever pray.

DOCUMENT 14.2 | LOTTIE ROLLIN, *Address on Universal Suffrage* (1870)

For some black women in South Carolina, Reconstruction offered the opportunity to agitate for a true universal suffrage—one that included blacks and whites, women and men. Three African American sisters—Charlotte (Lottie), Frances, and Louisa Rollin—mobilized for voting rights. Lottie Rollin gave the following address at a women's rights convention in Columbia, South Carolina, in 1870.

It had been so universally the custom to treat the idea of woman suffrage with ridicule and merriment that it becomes necessary in submitting the subject for earnest deliberation that we assure the gentlemen present that our claim is made honestly and seriously. We ask suffrage not as a favor, not as a privilege, but as a right based on the ground that we are human beings, and as such, entitled to all human rights. While we concede that woman's ennobling influence should be confined chiefly to home and society, we claim that public opinion has had a tendency to limit woman's sphere to too small a circle, and until woman has the right of representation this will last, and other rights will be held by an insecure tenure.

Source: Elizabeth Cady Stanton, Susan B. Anthony, and Matilda Joslyn Gage, eds., *History of Woman Suffrage*, vol. 3, *1876–1885* (Rochester: Susan B. Anthony, 1886), 828.

DOCUMENT 14.3 | ROBERT BROWN ELLIOTT, *In Defense of the Civil Rights Bill* (1874)

The English-born politician Robert Brown Elliott held a number of local and state offices in South Carolina during Reconstruction. He also became one of seven black members of the U.S. Congress when he won election to the House of Representatives in 1870. Elliott was a champion of black rights at each stage of his political career. On January 6, 1874, he gave the following address before Congress in defense of what would become the Civil Rights Act of 1875. In this excerpt, he counters Georgia senator Alexander Stephens's argument for states' rights.

Source: Alice Moore Dunbar, ed., *Masterpieces of Negro Eloquence: The Best Speeches Delivered by the Negro from the Days of Slavery to the Present Time* (New York: The Bookery Publishing Company, 1914), 67–70, 81–82, 85–87.

Mr. Speaker:

While I am sincerely grateful for this high mark of courtesy that has been accorded to me by this House, it is a matter of regret to me that it is necessary at this day that I should rise in the presence of an American Congress to advocate a bill which simply asserts equal rights and equal public privileges for all classes of American citizens. I regret, sir, that the dark hue of my skin may lend a color to the imputation that I am controlled by motives personal to myself in my advocacy of this great measure of national justice. Sir, the motive that impels me is restricted by no such narrow boundary, but is as broad as your Constitution. I advocate it, sir, because it is right. The bill, however, not only appeals to your justice, but it demands a response from your gratitude.

In the events that led to the achievement of American independence the Negro was not an inactive or unconcerned spectator. He bore his part bravely upon many battlefields, although uncheered by that certain hope of political elevation which victory would secure to the white man. The tall granite shaft, which a grateful State has reared above its sons who fell in defending Fort Griswold against the attack of Benedict Arnold, bears the name of Jordan, Freeman, and other brave men of the African race, who there cemented with their blood the corner-stone of the Republic. In the State which I have the honor in part to represent (South Carolina) the rifle of the black man rang out against the troops of the British Crown in the darkest days of the American Revolution. Said General Greene, who has been justly termed the "Washington of the North," in a letter written by him to Alexander Hamilton, on the 10th of January, 1781, from the vicinity of Camden, South Carolina: "There is no such thing as national character or national sentiment. The inhabitants are numerous, but they would be rather formidable abroad than at home. There is a great spirit of enterprise among the black people, and those that come out as volunteers are not a little formidable to the enemy."

At the battle of New Orleans under the immortal Jackson, a colored regiment held the extreme right of the American line unflinchingly, and drove back the British column that pressed upon them at the point of the bayonet. . . .

But, sir, we are told by the distinguished gentleman from Georgia (Mr. Stephens) that Congress has no power under the Constitution to pass such a law, and that the passage of such an act is in direct contravention of the rights of the States. I cannot assent to any such proposition. The Constitution of a free government ought always to be construed in favor of human rights. Indeed, the thirteenth, fourteenth, and fifteenth amendments, in positive words, invest Congress with the power to protect the citizen in his civil and political rights. Now, sir, what are civil rights? Rights natural, modified by civil society. . . .

When, therefore, the honorable gentleman from Georgia lends his voice and influence to defeat this measure, I do not shrink from saying that it is not from him that the American House of Representatives should take lessons in matters touching human rights or the joint relations of the State and national governments. . . .

Sir, it is scarcely twelve years since that gentleman shocked the civilized world by announcing the birth of a government which rested on human slavery as its cornerstone. The progress of events has swept away that pseudo-government which rested on greed, pride, and tyranny; and the race whom he then ruthlessly spurned and trampled on is here to meet him in debate, and to demand that the rights which are enjoyed by its former oppressors—who vainly sought to overthrow a Government which they could not prostitute to the base uses of slavery—shall be accorded to those who even in the darkness of slavery kept their allegiance true to freedom and the Union. Sir, the gentleman from Georgia has learned much since 1861; but he is still a laggard. . . .

Technically, this bill is to decide upon the civil status of the colored American citizen; a point disputed at the very formation of our present form of government, when by a short-sighted policy, a policy repugnant to true republican government, one Negro counted as three-fifths of a man. The logical result of this mistake of the framers of the Constitution strengthened the cancer of slavery, which finally spread its poisonous tentacles over the southern portion of the body politic. To arrest its growth and save the nation we have passed through the harrowing operation of intestine war, dreaded at all times, resorted to at the last extremity, like the surgeon's knife, but absolutely necessary to extirpate the disease which threatened with the life of the nation the overthrow of civil and political liberty on this continent. In that dire extremity the members of the race which I have the honor in part to represent—the race which pleads for justice at your hands to-day,—forgetful of their inhuman and brutalizing servitude at the South, their degradation and ostracism at the North, flew willingly and gallantly to the support of the national Government.

Their sufferings, assistance, privations, and trials in the swamps and in the rice-fields, their valor on the land and on the sea, form a part of the ever-glorious record which makes up the history of a nation preserved, and might, should I urge the claim, incline you to respect and guarantee their rights and privileges as citizens of our common Republic. But I remember that valor, devotion, and loyalty are not always rewarded according to their just deserts, and that after the battle some who have borne the brunt of the fray may, through neglect or contempt, be assigned to a subordinate place, while the enemies in war may be preferred to the sufferers.

The results of the war, as seen in reconstruction, have settled forever the political status of my race. The passage of this bill will determine the civil status, not only of the Negro, but of any other class of citizens who may feel themselves discriminated against. It will form the cap-stone of that temple of liberty, begun on this continent under discouraging circumstances, carried on in spite of the sneers of monarchists and the cavils of pretended friends of freedom, until at last it stands, in all its beautiful symmetry and proportions, a building the grandest which the world has ever seen, realizing the most sanguine expectations and the highest hopes of those who, in the name of equal, impartial, and universal liberty, laid the foundation-stone.

DOCUMENT 14.4 | JAMES SHEPHERD PIKE,
The Prostrate State (1874)

Throughout the 1870s, some northern writers lost enthusiasm and faith in Reconstruction. James Shepherd Pike, a Maine Republican, had supported Radical Reconstruction. In 1874, however, he published *The Prostrate State*, in which he argued that Reconstruction in South Carolina had failed. In the following excerpt, Pike describes his thoughts on South Carolina's interracial government.

Here, then, is the outcome, the ripe, perfected fruit of the boasted civilization of the South, after two hundred years of experience. A white community, that had gradually risen from small beginnings, till it grew into wealth, culture, and refinement, and became accomplished in all the arts of civilization; that successfully asserted its resistance to a foreign tyranny by deeds of conspicuous valor, which achieved liberty and independence through the fire and tempest of civil war, and illustrated itself in the councils of the nation by orators and statesmen worthy of any age or nation—such a community is then reduced to this. It lies prostrate in the dust, ruled over by this strange conglomerate, gathered from the ranks of its own servile population. It is the spectacle of a society suddenly turned bottom-side up. The wealth, the intelligence, the culture, the wisdom of the State, have broken through the crust of that social volcano on which they were contentedly reposing, and have sunk out of sight, consumed by the subterranean fires they had with such temerity braved and defied.

In the place of this old aristocratic society stands the rude form of the most ignorant democracy that mankind ever saw, invested with the functions of government. It is the dregs of the population habilitated in the robes of their intelligent predecessors, and asserting over them the rule of ignorance and corruption, through the inexorable machinery of a majority of numbers. It is barbarism overwhelming civilization by physical force. It is the slave rioting in the halls of his master, and putting that master under his feet. And, though it is done without malice and without vengeance, it is nevertheless none the less completely and absolutely done. Let us approach nearer and take a closer view. We will enter the House of Representatives. Here sit one hundred and twenty-four members. Of these, twenty-three are white men, representing the remains of the old civilization. These are good-looking, substantial citizens. They are men of weight and standing in the communities they represent. They are all from the hill country. The frosts of sixty and seventy winters whiten the heads of some among them. There they sit, grim and silent. They feel themselves to be but loose stones, thrown in to partially obstruct a current they are powerless to resist. . . .

Deducting the twenty-three members referred to, who comprise the entire strength of the opposition, we find one hundred and one remaining. Of this one hundred and one, ninety-four are colored, and seven are their white allies. Thus the

Source: James Shepherd Pike, *The Prostrate State: South Carolina under Negro Government* (New York: D. Appleton and Company, 1874), 11–15.

blacks outnumber the whole body of whites in the House more than three to one. On the mere basis of numbers in the State the injustice of this disproportion is manifest, since the black population is relatively four to three of the whites. A just rectification of the disproportion, on the basis of population merely, would give fifty-four whites to seventy black members. And the line of race very nearly marks the line of hostile politics. As things stand, the body is almost literally a Black Parliament, and it is the only one on the face of the earth which is the representative of a white constituency and the professed exponent of an advanced type of modern civilization.

DOCUMENT 14.5 | ULYSSES S. GRANT, *Letter to South Carolina Governor D. H. Chamberlain* (1876)

On July 8, 1876, racial violence erupted in the small, all-black town of Hamburg, South Carolina. A black militia unit there clashed with whites from nearby communities. Six blacks and one white died in the fighting. The so-called Hamburg Massacre boosted the Democrats' campaign argument that "Republican Rule" had led to racial violence. Republican governor D. H. Chamberlain appealed to President Grant for assistance. Grant's reply signaled the federal government's retreat from Reconstruction.

Washington, July 26, 1876

Dear Sir:

I am in receipt of your letter of the 22d of July, and all the enclosures enumerated therein, giving an account of the late barbarous massacre of innocent men at the town of Hamburg, S.C. The views which you express as to the duty you owe to your oath of office and to the citizens to secure to all their civil rights, including the right to vote according to the dictates of their own consciences, and the further duty of the Executive of the nation to give all needful aid, when properly called on to do so, to enable you to ensure this inalienable right, I fully concur in.

The scene at Hamburg, as cruel, bloodthirsty, wanton, unprovoked, and as uncalled for as it was, is only a repetition of the course that has been pursued in other States within the last few years, notably in Mississippi and Louisiana. Mississippi is governed to-day by officials chosen through fraud and violence, such as would scarcely be accredited to savages, much less to a civilized and Christian people. How long these things are to continue, or what is to be the final remedy, the Great Ruler of the Universe only knows; but I have an abiding faith that the remedy will come, and come speedily, and I earnestly hope that it will come peacefully. There has never been a desire on the part of the North to humiliate the South; nothing is claimed for one State that is not freely accorded to all the others, unless it may be the right to kill negroes and Republicans without fear of punishment and without loss of caste or reputation. This has seemed to be a privilege claimed by a few States.

Source: Edward McPherson, *A Handbook of Politics for 1876* (Washington, D.C.: Solomons and Chapman, 1876), 207.

I repeat again, that I fully agree with you as to the measure of your duties in the present emergency, and as to my duties. Go on, and let every Governor, where the same dangers threaten the peace of his State, go on in the conscientious discharge of his duties to the humblest as well as the proudest citizen, and I will give every aid for which I can find law or constitutional power. A government that cannot give protection to the life, property, and all guaranteed civil rights (in this country the greatest is an untrammeled ballot) to the citizen is, in so far, a failure, and every energy of the oppressed should be exerted (always within the law and by constitutional means) to regain lost privileges or protection.

Too long denial of guaranteed rights is sure to lead to revolution, bloody revolution, where suffering must fall upon the innocent as well as the guilty. Expressing the hope that the better judgment and co-operation of citizens of the State over which you have presided so ably may enable you to secure a fair trial, and punishment of all offenders without distinction of race, color, or previous condition of servitude, and without aid from the Federal Government, but with the promise of such aid on the conditions named in the foregoing, I subscribe myself very respectfully your obedient servant,

U. S. Grant.

INTERPRET THE EVIDENCE

1. What did the Colored People's Convention of South Carolina demand in the months after the end of the war (Document 14.1)? How did the participants justify their arguments?

2. According to Lottie Rollin, why do women deserve the right to vote (Document 14.2)? How does she appeal to traditional gender norms in making this argument?

3. How does Robert Brown Elliott cite history in defense of the Civil Rights Bill (Document 14.3)? Why did blacks deserve the equal rights of citizenship? How does Elliott discredit Stephens's arguments?

4. According to James Shepherd Pike, what was wrong with South Carolina's government (Document 14.4)? How does he describe the black members of the South Carolina legislature? The white members?

5. How did President Grant respond to D. H. Chamberlain's request for protection from violence against blacks and white Republicans (Document 14.5)? Does he offer any assistance? What is his outlook on the future of racial tension in the South?

6. According to the Colored People's Convention, Rollin, and Elliott, what constituted equal citizenship for African Americans?

PUT IT IN CONTEXT

1. How do Pike's book and Grant's reply to Governor Chamberlain show how Republicans in the North backed away from Reconstruction?